The Epic: A Very Short Introduction

VERY SHORT INTRODUCTIONS are for anyone wanting a stimulating and accessible way into a new subject. They are written by experts, and have been translated into more than 45 different languages.

The series began in 1995, and now covers a wide variety of topics in every discipline. The VSI library currently contains over 750 volumes—a Very Short Introduction to everything from Psychology and Philosophy of Science to American History and Relativity—and continues to grow in every subject area.

Very Short Introductions available now:

ANALYTIC PHILOSOPHY
Michael Beaney
ANARCHISM Alex Prichard
ANCIENT ASSYRIA Karen Radner
ANCIENT EGYPT Ian Shaw
ANCIENT EGYPTIAN ART AND
ARCHITECTURE Christina Riggs
ANCIENT GREECE Paul Cartledge
ANCIENT GREEK AND ROMAN
SCIENCE Liba Taub
THE ANCIENT NEAR EAST
Amanda H. Podany
ANCIENT PHILOSOPHY Julia Annas
ANCIENT WARFARE
Harry Sidebottom
ANGELS David Albert Jones
ANGLICANISM Mark Chapman
THE ANGLO-SAXON AGE John Blair
ANIMAL BEHAVIOUR
Tristram D. Wyatt
THE ANIMAL KINGDOM
Peter Holland
ANIMAL RIGHTS David DeGrazia
ANSELM Thomas Williams
THE ANTARCTIC Klaus Dodds
ANTHROPOCENE Erle C. Ellis
ANTISEMITISM Steven Beller
ANXIETY Daniel Freeman and
Jason Freeman
THE APOCRYPHAL GOSPELS
Paul Foster
APPLIED MATHEMATICS
Alain Goriely
THOMAS AQUINAS Fergus Kerr
ARBITRATION Thomas Schultz and
Thomas Grant
ARCHAEOLOGY Paul Bahn
ARCHITECTURE Andrew Ballantyne
THE ARCTIC Klaus Dodds and
Jamie Woodward
HANNAH ARENDT Dana Villa
ARISTOCRACY William Doyle
ARISTOTLE Jonathan Barnes
ART HISTORY Dana Arnold
ART THEORY Cynthia Freeland
ARTIFICIAL INTELLIGENCE
Margaret A. Boden
ASIAN AMERICAN HISTORY
Madeline Y. Hsu
ASTROBIOLOGY David C. Catling

ASTROPHYSICS James Binney
ATHEISM Julian Baggini
THE ATMOSPHERE Paul I. Palmer
AUGUSTINE Henry Chadwick
JANE AUSTEN Tom Keymer
AUSTRALIA Kenneth Morgan
AUTHORITARIANISM James Loxton
AUTISM Uta Frith
AUTOBIOGRAPHY Laura Marcus
THE AVANT GARDE David Cottington
THE AZTECS David Carrasco
BABYLONIA Trevor Bryce
BACTERIA Sebastian G. B. Amyes
BANKING John Goddard and
John O. S. Wilson
BARTHES Jonathan Culler
THE BEATS David Sterritt
BEAUTY Roger Scruton
LUDWIG VAN BEETHOVEN
Mark Evan Bonds
BEHAVIOURAL ECONOMICS
Michelle Baddeley
BESTSELLERS John Sutherland
THE BIBLE John Riches
BIBLICAL ARCHAEOLOGY Eric H. Cline
BIG DATA Dawn E. Holmes
BIOCHEMISTRY Mark Lorch
BIODIVERSITY CONSERVATION
David Macdonald
BIOGEOGRAPHY Mark V. Lomolino
BIOGRAPHY Hermione Lee
BIOMETRICS Michael Fairhurst
ELIZABETH BISHOP Jonathan F. S. Post
BLACK HOLES Katherine Blundell
BLASPHEMY Yvonne Sherwood
BLOOD Chris Cooper
THE BLUES Elijah Wald
THE BODY Chris Shilling
THE BOHEMIANS David Weir
NIELS BOHR J. L. Heilbron
THE BOOK OF COMMON PRAYER
Brian Cummings
THE BOOK OF MORMON
Terryl Givens
BORDERS Alexander C. Diener and
Joshua Hagen
THE BRAIN Michael O'Shea
BRANDING Robert Jones
THE BRICS Andrew F. Cooper
BRITISH ARCHITECTURE Dana Arnold

Available soon:

(to be confirmed)

For more information visit our website
www.oup.com/vsi/

Anthony Welch

THE EPIC

A Very Short Introduction

OXFORD
UNIVERSITY PRESS

OXFORD
UNIVERSITY PRESS

Great Clarendon Street, Oxford, OX2 6DP,
United Kingdom

Oxford University Press is a department of the University of Oxford.
It furthers the University's objective of excellence in research, scholarship,
and education by publishing worldwide. Oxford is a registered trade mark of
Oxford University Press in the UK and in certain other countries

Published in the United States of America by Oxford University Press
198 Madison Avenue, New York, NY 10016, United States of America

British Library Cataloguing in Publication Data
Data available

Library of Congress Control Number: 2024936044

ISBN 978-0-19-879512-4

Printed and bound by
CPI Group (UK) Ltd, Croydon, CR0 4YY

Links to third party websites are provided by Oxford in good faith and
for information only. Oxford disclaims any responsibility for the materials
contained in any third party website referenced in this work.

Contents

Acknowledgments

Writing this little book has been something of an epic endeavor: a journey fraught with delays and mischances, strange encounters in far-flung scholarly fields, and even a perilous sojourn in the underworld of university administration. I am grateful to the VSI editors, Andrea Keegan, Jenny Nugée, and Luciana O'Flaherty, and their team for guiding this project with heroic patience and good cheer. I extend my thanks, too, to my anonymous readers for Oxford University Press. I gratefully acknowledge the financial support of the Denbo Center for Humanities and the Arts at the University of Tennessee, where I began the research for this book as a faculty fellow in residence. All my work on epic literature owes profound debts to my teachers David Quint and John Leonard, who introduced me to the European epic tradition. This book has also benefited from my conversations with Ayesha Ramachandran, Sarah Van der Laan, Roy Liuzza, Joshua Scodel, and Tobias Gregory. As always, I owe my deepest gratitude to Heather Hirschfeld, my steadfast companion on the road of adventure.

List of illustrations

Chapter 1
A story of all things

What is an epic?

The title of this book might raise an eyebrow. What can be very short about the epic? The word conjures up immensity, grandeur, girth. The epic is the only literary form that we define first and foremost by its weight, like an Olympic boxer or a flank steak. Like any large organism, epics are also bewilderingly diverse. They have evolved in endless ways to thrive in far-flung habitats, from Iceland and Siberia to Sri Lanka and Central Africa. Can a little book contain them all? Of course not. Yet the world's epic traditions have much in common, and together they tell an important part of our human story. The goal of this very short introduction is to survey the rich variety of epic storytelling around the globe, but also to trace some deep resemblances that might tell us why the epic has mattered to so many for so long.

What is an epic? In popular usage, it is a label for all things oversized or grandiose: an epic vacation; an epic hangover. Let us turn to our literary handbooks for a more technical definition. They inform us that the epic is a long narrative poem about the deeds of heroes. Its diction is lofty and formulaic. Its formal conventions include the poet's invocation of a god or muse, lengthy catalogues, protracted similes, and ornate descriptions of art objects. The epic hero undertakes a war or a quest that calls for extraordinary gifts of body and mind. Supernatural forces aid or resist the hero's work. Taking place in a legendary heroic age, the epic's plot is nonlinear, beginning *in medias res*, in the midst of the action, and then unfolding past and future events through retrospective narration or prophecy. The epic poet relies on a stockpile of traditional scene types, which might include single combats, shipwrecks, feasts, animal sacrifices, war councils, and journeys to the underworld.

As we close our handbooks, a problem lingers in our minds. Pulling more volumes from the shelf, we soon amass a large pile of European epic poems that lack some of those defining traits. Our disquiet swells into full-blown panic when we turn to heroic traditions in the world beyond Europe. In this strange wilderness—much of it reconnoitred by Western scholars only in the last few decades—lurk lion men and buffalo women, flying horses and talking birds, monster-slaying children, shape-shifting demons, magical diseases and miraculous births, cataclysmic battles, and harrowing cosmic journeys. The more widely we read, the flimsier our definitions seem to us. And no wonder, for they are based on a tiny selection of European masterpieces. It is as if a marine biologist tried to classify the world's ocean life by studying a pond of prized goldfish. Our trusty handbooks have failed us, in other words, because the literary conventions that Western readers once thought to be timeless and universal now look like a tangled knot of local accidents.

The most crucial of those accidents is named Homer. The *Iliad* and *Odyssey* probably came into being somewhere along the western coastline of Asia Minor in the 8th century BCE. In those early days, the Greeks' oral traditions were an art without a name; poets simply called them *aoidai* (songs) or *mûthoi* (stories). Not until the 5th century BCE did writers like Herodotus and Pindar start using a different word, *epos* (word, speech, tale), for certain kinds of hexameter poetry about gods and heroes. As literacy spread across the Greek-speaking world, scholars slowly fashioned those ancient folk stories into a literary canon. Poetry was arranged into a system of genres with strict rules and conventions. Authors were judged, compared, and ranked. Formal schemes of rhetoric and poetics arose. Slowly, over centuries, the literary form known today as the epic was born, made in the image of those great Homeric songs about the Trojan War.

When the Romans absorbed the literary culture of Hellenistic Greece, the *Iliad* and *Odyssey* became blueprints for Rome's own canon of heroic poetry. Homer's memory lingered in nearly every line of Virgil's great Latin masterwork, the *Aeneid* (*c*.19 BCE)—and the *Aeneid*, in turn, was to be the most influential poem in the Western world for the next 2,000 years. From the grammar schools of Shakespeare's England to the Parisian salons of Voltaire and Montesquieu to the nerve centres of European colonial rule from Lima to New Delhi, cultural literacy meant knowing Virgil's *Aeneid* and the poetic tradition it had spawned. As the poem's influence spiralled outward from its Roman homeland, slowly coiling around the globe in endless chains of literary imitation, still encoded in its DNA was the ancient legacy of the Homeric epics. And so a handful of Bronze Age war stories, told and retold by wandering singers on the coasts of the Aegean Sea, still defines this art form for millions of readers today.

An epic, then, in this narrow but important sense, is a literary work modelled on the long narrative poems of Homer and Virgil. But an epic is more than a patchwork of ancient literary conventions. These are stories about grand achievements, won at the cost of pain and sacrifice. They show the human will pushing against resistance, risking everything to leave a lasting mark on the universe. Bold youths clutch at glory in the dust and heat of the battlefield. Kingdoms rise and burn to ashes. Mortals quarrel with the gods and dare to touch the sky. Stories like these are told all over the world, many springing from oral traditions that look much like Homer's. Yet can we really label them epics, a word unknown to the storytellers who made them? Should all these

3

artworks bear the name of a literary form that originated in Greece and Rome?

These are hard questions, not least because the Western epic has a long history of nationalist and colonial designs. Virgil's *Aeneid* taught first the Romans, and then the fledgling nations of Europe, that the epic could be a powerful tool of political identity. Virgil's hero, Aeneas, was the legendary founder of the Roman Empire. In his adventures, Roman readers saw the rise of a people destined to conquer the world. Epic poetry would later become a sword of holy war against Islam during the Crusades; a cudgel to bludgeon fellow Christians in the European wars of religion; a scourge wielded by conquistadors and colonizers around the globe. In due time, the epic also absorbed the ethnic nationalism of the Romantic era. Western philosophers like Vico, Rousseau, and Hegel came to believe that the oldest epics they knew, Homer's *Iliad* and *Odyssey*, were not the work of a single artist but a mysterious outgrowth of the Greek national spirit, sprouting organically, like wildflowers, from the rustic folk traditions of Homer's countrymen. Gathering up their maps and notebooks, scholars hiked into the European backwoods in hopes of finding their own lost Homers in the Scottish Highlands or Finland's lake district.

Within a generation or two, fieldworkers had taken the search outside Europe. Wherever they found indigenous oral traditions that looked vaguely Homeric, that old word *epos* rose to their lips. The Romantic philosophers had described the archaic Greeks as a childlike race, innocent and wild; it was all too easy to project the same primitivist fantasies onto non-European cultures. Library shelves began to fill with the so-called epics of West African villagers, nomadic herders in Central Asia, and fishing communities in northern Japan. Many societies had seemingly experienced their own heroic ages, fought their own Trojan Wars, and poured their own ethnic spirit into epic songs. Only recently, as Western colonial power has slowly relaxed its grip on the world's peoples, have scholars learned to put away their Homeric templates and to treat non-European cultural forms on their own terms.

Is there no such thing, then, as global epic literature? Not in the narrow sense we have considered so far. If we use the Greco-Roman epic as a one-size-fits-all blueprint for the literary arts of Ossetia, Mali, and Tamil Nadu, then we are little better than those early European explorers who thought the giraffe and the llama were merely oddly shaped horses. Many specialists do view the Western epic as just one of many distinct, incommensurate heroic traditions around the world, each with its own name and local history. We might simply lay them all side by side—*epic, dastan, jer, bylina, mvet, wasala, kárisi*, and a hundred more—and despair of studying them as a worldwide family of cognate literary forms. But this would snatch away our chance to explore the many striking affinities they share. It might also imply that non-European storytelling does not deserve the prestigious name of epic, as if it were only fit for anthropologists or folklorists, not for students of great literature. For that matter, the Homeric epics themselves owe debts to much older oral traditions that stretched across the ancient Near East—and perhaps even spiderwebbed all over the prehistoric Indo-European world. The epic has always been cosmopolitan, a genre on the move. We should keep in mind that literary genres are not fixed laws of nature but ongoing negotiations, a consensus that changes over time. What we need is a more inclusive definition of the epic as a global art form. So let us try again.

World epics: six family traits

What is an epic? Since we have a global horizon in view, we shall need to look past superficial features of form and style. New questions come into focus: Why were these stories made? For whom? What deep structures do they share? In brief, here are six traits that describe the epic texts and traditions surveyed in this book.

First, the epic is a traditional and communal art. It is defined less by its literary *form* than by its social *function*. Epics nourish a sense of group identity. Whether chanted aloud in a village square or printed for silent reading, their stories preserve the cultural heritage that binds a society together. They bear witness to a people's memories, experiences, and values. They link their audience members to one another and to their ancestors in a shared act of imagination. Over time, these stories coalesce into epic traditions, which are sustained by the careful imitation of prior models. Epics can take many different forms because each is built to serve the unique needs of its community.

Second, epics employ a distinct literary style. Their formal artistry, like their subject matter, is traditional; it tends to spring from techniques of oral performance, which rely on repetition and ritual. This means that epic language typically has a stylized, formulaic quality. Although epic styles vary widely across cultures, they are usually heightened in some way, composed in an artificial language that rises above everyday talk. Its ceremonial dignity shows that the story being told is old and precious. Yet each artist who retells the old stories still claims a measure of creative freedom, like a master chef reworking a classic recipe. Every text, every performance is a unique blend of imitation and originality, tradition and independence.

Third, with few exceptions, epics are hero stories. They narrate the deeds of special human beings who are born into greatness. Paradoxically, the stories of these singular heroes, standing apart from all the rest, often speak to the collective norms and aspirations of a society. Sometimes the epic hero is a shining exemplar to be admired and emulated. But only sometimes. Their doings are not always praiseworthy. They matter because, for better or worse, they make a lasting impact on their community. Epics are not psychological novels; their heroes' personalities are often shallow and crudely drawn. What they do share is an extraordinary force of will. They know what they want and try to

6

attain it at a high cost. It is their actions that count, striving to make the world answer to their demands. Let us add that this book will not address the long scientific, philosophical, and religious poems that Western readers sometimes call didactic epics; we are concerned with heroic narratives.

Fourth, epics are archives. Although they showcase the deeds of great heroes, epics have evolved into storage systems that stockpile a society's traditional knowledge. This is why they so often arise from oral cultures, which use storytelling to transmit valuable information across space and time in the absence of writing. Epics can act as encyclopedias or how-to manuals of religion and cosmology, geography and ethnography, kinship and marriage, social institutions, political history, genealogical lore, and customary practices such as hunting, warfare, or sacrifice. As vessels of tradition, epics honor the past. Many of their stories take place long ago, in a bright, flamboyant heroic age. However, the epic sometimes shadows the glories of the past with questioning and doubt, as if drifting in and out of its own idealizing dreams.

Fifth, epics are typically grounded in history but portray a supernatural cosmos. Epics tend to emerge in traditional cultures that do not make tidy distinctions between literature, history, and myth. Often calling the hero away from civilization into the wilderness, epics move along the outer periphery of human experience, bordering on other forms of being: the bestial, the godly, the demonic. Some epic heroes are the human avatars of gods. Others journey to the lands of the dead or tap into magical energies that grant them godlike powers. Yet they are not the otherworldly supermen of myth and legend. Their feet remain on the ground. Epics generally tell stories that their audiences believe (or at least half-believe) to have really happened. They often depict important historical events, such as wars or migrations. Although tantalizingly close to divinity, epic heroes are human beings like ourselves, conscious of weakness and loss, aching under the burden of mortality.

It might come as a surprise that we have left out the epic's best-known trait: its length. In fact, size is not a very reliable litmus test. Samuel Richardson's bulky novel *Clarissa* weighs in at nearly one million words. Few readers would call it a heroic epic. Yet many would bestow that title on the Old English *Beowulf*, a lean, muscular poem of fewer than 18,000 words. Indeed, the Homeric *Iliad* (roughly 15,500 verses) and *Odyssey* (12,100 verses) are longer than most European epic poems, if we set aside a few outliers such as the bulging chivalric epics of Renaissance Italy. The French *chansons de geste*, the Russian *byliny*, the Middle High German heroic poems, the South Slavic oral epics first transcribed by American fieldworkers in the 1930s—all of these typically range from 1,000 to 12,000 lines. Many oral epics from West Africa to Southeast Asia fall within the same range. Then again, the Homeric poems look like newspaper clippings when compared to the Indian *Mahābhārata*, with more than 100,000 couplet verses in some of its recensions. And even that colossal Sanskrit epic is dwarfed by the oral storytelling traditions of North and Central Asia. One *Gesar* singer's repertoire, transcribed by scholars at the University of Tibet, includes a jaw-dropping 600,000 lines of poetry—the equivalent of nearly 200 *Beowulf*s. Length alone does not tell the whole story.

All this word counting is really an effort to highlight something else that the world's epics share, something harder to quantify. Our sixth trait is *comprehensiveness*. Epics are built on a large scale. Spacious and grandiose, they describe momentous human affairs: wars, quests, revolutions, confrontations with gods and monsters, journeys of pilgrimage or homecoming. Events like these have consequences that ripple across history, and sometimes across the cosmos. As public archives, epics are inclusive and agglomerative. In their leisurely fullness of vision, they ponder family and kinship, politics, justice, religion, ethics, art, and death. They want to tell you who the hero's great-grandparents were, and why serpents shed their skin, and what strange flowers bloom on the far slope of some distant hill. Big, slow, and sturdy, epics are not constructed for speed but for hauling freight.

In their quest for comprehensiveness, epics often absorb other literary forms into themselves. They may contain laments, prayers, love songs, praise poems, myths and etiologies, riddles, proverbs, and more. Scholars sometimes describe the epic as a master genre that includes all the rest. A deep form, some call it; a superstory. Maybe that is why, in many cultures, there is no distinct word for the epic. In ancient Greek, as we saw earlier, *epos* means word or saying. In parts of Central Asia, an oral epic is known as a *destan* or *dastan*, deriving from a Persian word for a story or tale. The *sagas* of medieval Iceland and Norway derive their name from the Old Norse verb *segja*, to say or tell. In the Mandinka region of West Africa, a long oral narrative is often called *tariko* or *tariku*, from the Arabic word *ta'rikh* (history), while certain epics bear the name *maana* (from Arabic *macna*, meaning). Word, saying, story, history. The epic is almost synonymous with storytelling itself: a story of all things.

Instead of surveying the world's epics in a strictly chronological or geographical arrangement, this book takes a thematic approach. Using the above list of traits as a point of departure, each chapter highlights some common features of the epic as a global literary form, with representative examples from a wide variety of cultural traditions. Although the masterpieces of the Western epic canon loom large throughout, our global framework will allow broader cross-cultural family traits to emerge. Let us sally forth, then, on our own heroic quest to measure the vast range and heft of this ancient art form, lovingly preserved on clay tablets, papyrus, palm leaf, and vellum, and on the lips of oral poets all over the world.

Chapter 2
The singer and the song

On 20 December 1853, Hormuzd Rassam made a breathtaking discovery. For weeks, his team had been excavating the remains of an ancient palace at Nineveh, near his birthplace in Mosul, Iraq. The British Museum had sent Rassam to the region in search of rare antiquities. He had followed his keen instincts to this spot, not far from a site explored a few years earlier by his mentor, the English archaeologist Austen Henry Layard. On this winter night, Rassam's men first began to unearth the palace library of Ashurbanipal, the last great king of the waning Neo-Assyrian Empire. The imperial palace had been sacked in 612 BCE, and its famous library had been lost for centuries under the sands.

In the weeks that followed, the men dug deeper into the complex. Piles of clay tablets lay broken and buried in the ruins. These shards of clay bore little furrows of wedge-shaped letter forms, the ancient script that Western scholars had named *cuneiform* (from the Latin word *cuneus*, wedge). Written on some of the tablets were poems composed in the long-dead Akkadian language. Among them, damaged and unintelligible, was the literary masterpiece that is now called the *Epic of Gilgamesh*. It told the story of a mighty Sumerian king, a monster slayer who spurned the love of a goddess and vainly sought eternal life. Rassam grasped none of this; deciphering the unknown script would take decades.

Nor could he know that this astonishing poem was far older than the palace complex his men had won back from the earth. Archaeologists have since found versions of the Gilgamesh story that were written down almost 4,000 years ago. They formed part of a vast Bronze Age literary culture across the Near East, a common heritage of hero tales and creation myths that once stretched from Egypt to the Iranian Plateau, from the Persian Gulf to the Black Sea. The distant watersheds of this great sea of stories include the Homeric epics and the Hebrew Bible.

When we think of epic poetry, many of us picture these relics exhumed from old libraries. We imagine fired clay tablets, papyrus scrolls, worm-eaten manuscripts. Yet few of the world's epic traditions have been preserved in writing at all. The most popular medium of epic storytelling has always been the human voice. Epic singers thrived in countless societies before the rise of literacy. Some still sing today. Many cultures have given these performers special names to mark their privileged social roles: *biwa hōshi*, *dastanči*, *griot*, *guslar*, *kárisi*, *manaschi*, *rhapsode*, *scop*, *skald*. Their artistry has much in common around the globe and across time. Even the literary epics of Western Europe, long confined to the printed page, have been shaped in many ways by their origins in speech and song.

The world's traditional oral epics are not timebound artifacts. They are evolving organisms, rooted in living ecosystems of culture and tradition. In an oral community, a performer rarely recites a long heroic tale—*Beowulf*, say, or *The Wedding of Smailagić Meho*—at one sitting. Instead, the epic singer will extract one or more episodes from a common reservoir of traditional heroic legends. Some of those legends might cluster around a single character (such as Sunjata, the West African culture hero) or a significant event (such as the fall of Troy). An evening's performance might focus on the hero's childhood. Another might linger over a great battle. All these recitals, with their endless minor variations, form a shared *macrotext*, a mesh of interconnected stories that constitutes an oral epic tradition. Some versions of those tales happen to get written down and, over time, harden into fixed, authoritative texts. Others fade from view. From this vast ancient ocean of unwritten heroic tales arose the earliest ancestors of the *Iliads* and *Beowulfs* that line our bookshelves today.

Homeric epic: from song to text

Many of the world's literary epics sprang from oral traditions. So how exactly did they turn into written texts? The Homeric epics offer valuable clues. The stories told in the *Iliad* and *Odyssey* are set in the world of Mycenaean Greece (*c.*1600–1100 BCE), a late Bronze Age civilization that encircled the Aegean Sea like a necklace of bright sea stones. The Mycenaeans were maritime merchants who built sprawling trade networks across the Mediterranean Sea. For the bureaucratic work of government and commerce they developed a writing system, the syllabic script known as Linear B, which faded from use when the Mycenaean kingdoms mysteriously collapsed in the 12th century BCE. But memories of those prosperous days must have lingered in the songs of travelling bards in Greece and Asia Minor. Some of those tales later coalesced into a cycle of heroic legends about the Trojan War. Alongside the *Iliad* and *Odyssey*, the oral songs of the Epic Cycle came to bear such names as *Cypria*, *Aethiopis*, *Little Iliad*, and *Nostoi* (*Returns*). Only fragments of those lost stories survive.

In later times, Greek writers attributed two poems from the Trojan Cycle to a shadowy figure named Homer: the *Iliad*, narrating the Greek siege of Troy (a city also known as Ilion), and the *Odyssey*, tracing the Greek hero Odysseus' long journey home to Ithaca. Nothing certain is known about Homer, nor indeed whether he existed at all. Ancient biographers told of a blind bard living in the Greek-speaking settlements of Ionia, along the western coast of modern-day Turkey. Much of what we know about those archaic poet-singers (called *aoidoi*) comes from literary sources such as the *Odyssey*; we see Homer's self-portrait, perhaps,

in the blind court poet Demodocus, who moves Odysseus
to tears with his songs of the Trojan War.

Most scholars believe that the Homeric epics were composed in the
8th or early 7th century BCE. By this time, literacy was returning to
Greece in a new alphabetic script borrowed from Phoenician
traders. But it is not clear that singers or their audiences wanted to
write down the old heroic songs. From the 6th to the 3rd century
BCE, professional reciters and musicians known as *rhapsodoi* (tale
weavers, from the Greek terms *rhapto*, stitch, and *aoide*, song)
gathered to compete for prizes at religious festivals in the emerging
Greek city states, such as the annual Panathenaea in Athens. We
know that some *rhapsodoi* performed Homer's epics. They might
have relied on written texts, or they might simply have memorized
the *Iliad* and *Odyssey* by ear—an authorized oral edition, so to
speak, passed from one generation to the next—long before the
poems were set down in writing.

Eventually, written manuscripts of the Homeric poems began to
spread across Greece. Not until the 3rd century BCE were definitive
texts compiled by a small community of Greek scholars in northern
Egypt. Working in the great library of Alexandria, at this time the
foremost intellectual centre in the Mediterranean world, they
patiently assembled, collated, and edited some 27,000 lines of
Homeric poetry on papyrus scrolls. They also composed vast
editorial commentaries, known as *scholia*, that meticulously
analysed the poems' language, versification, style, and manuscript
variants, giving us precious insights into their textual history. It
was probably these Alexandrian editors who first divided the *Iliad*
and *Odyssey* into 24 books, one for each letter of the Greek
alphabet. The Homeric texts they crafted with such care are
essentially those we still read today.

The oral origins of these poems were gradually forgotten. In the
bookish ages to come, intellectuals could scarcely imagine Homer
composing poems of such artistic skill and scope without the tools

of literacy. Yet even after the Homeric epics found a home in ancient libraries, and eventually in the printing houses of early modern Europe, the notion of a nonliterate Homer never fully passed away. It took on new life in the 18th and 19th centuries, revived by Romantic primitivists who compared the *Iliad* and *Odyssey* to the oral folk poetry of their own nations. And so arose the great Homeric Question: What if these epics were not the work of a single literary author but a collective outpouring of many voices? In his *Prolegomena ad Homerum* (1795), the German classicist Friedrich August Wolf boldly concluded that the two Homeric epics were amalgams of many shorter poems, composed by untold numbers of anonymous, illiterate poets, that had circulated orally for centuries before they were stitched together to form the *Iliad* and *Odyssey*. But Wolf's powerful arguments left a deeper mystery unsolved. How could a society have produced such complex works of art without the aid of writing?

The making of oral-formulaic poetry

The mysterious origins of the *Iliad* and *Odyssey* eventually led scholars to a cluster of villages in the Balkans. In 1928, the American classicist Milman Parry had completed a doctoral thesis on the Homeric epics at the Sorbonne in Paris. His research explored the poems' repeated epithets or set phrases, which he called *formulae*: 'the wine-dark sea'; 'bright-eyed Athena'; 'the Trojans, tamers of horses'. These verbal formulae are oddly persistent and unchanging. Fully one-eighth of the *Iliad*'s 15,693 verses include a repeated formulaic phrase.

Parry's crucial insight was that those stock phrases played a key role in the rhythmic structure of Homeric poetry. The Homeric epics are composed in a metre known as dactylic hexameter. Each verse strings together recurring patterns of long and short syllables. Parry came to see that each Homeric formula— 'bright-eyed Athena' and the rest—is nearly always placed in the same metrical slots within the verse line. He discovered, in other words, that the endlessly repeated phrases in the *Iliad* and *Odyssey* were not due to lazy or primitive storytelling. Instead, they were somehow related to the underlying mechanics of Homeric verse rhythm, the structural logic of metre and form.

The last piece of the puzzle snapped into place when Parry, now teaching at Harvard University, realized that the formula was an ideal tool for composing oral poetry. In the early 1930s, he travelled to eastern Europe with his student, Albert Bates Lord, in search of oral performers who could allegedly recite long heroic poems without recourse to reading or writing. Parry and Lord soon encountered a living South Slavic oral tradition that transformed their understanding of Homeric poetry. Illiterate singers (called *guslari*) in the small towns of Yugoslavia, accompanying themselves on the one-stringed *gusle* and other lute-like instruments, were able to perform heroic songs of amazing length and complexity (see Figure 1). In summer 1935, for example, Parry's team recorded a dozen poems recited by Avdo Međedović, a butcher from eastern Montenegro. They amassed some 53 hours of sound recordings and transcriptions, sung at a rate of roughly 18–20 verses per minute. The longest of Međedović's oral poems was 13,331 verses. He claimed to have a repertoire of 58 heroic songs; other *guslari* knew as many as 70 or 80 poems. In all, Parry and Lord compiled more than 12,000 texts recited by traditional oral singers in the region.

The guslars did not strictly memorize their long poems. Rather, they used techniques of composition in performance that relied on both memory and improvisation. The performer largely composed his verses on the spot, but he made the task much easier for himself by sprinkling formulaic phrases into his poetry. The repeated formulae not only filled out the metrical needs of each verse, just as Homer's did, but also gave the singer a moment to ready himself for the next sprint of poetic invention. These formulae were traditional, forming a common lexicon that many singers shared over long periods of time.

1. The guslar Todor Visnjevac, photographed by Parry or Lord in Gacko, Bosnia and Herzegovina, in the early 1930s.

Parry and Lord speculated that the Homeric poems must have come into being in much the same way. Those infamous phrases—'swift-footed Achilles' and 'rosy-fingered dawn'—were a lingering residue of this nonliterate practice of *oral-formulaic composition*, still preserved in the Homeric texts like prehistoric life forms sealed in amber. This also explained why Homer sometimes used strangely archaic word forms or obscure dialects that puzzled modern linguists. Many of those words had become trapped within the bards' ancient storehouse of traditional poetic formulae, frozen in time, even as the Greek language changed around them. In much the same way, English nursery rhymes still cling to old-fashioned phrases like 'curds and whey' or 'a pocket full of rye'.

Formulaic phrases are not the only building blocks of oral epic poetry. Parry and Lord also noticed that both Homer and the South Slavic singers used recurring plot episodes or scene types in their poems. Over and over, the poet might describe a sunrise, a feast, a journey on horseback, a messenger's report, or the arming of a warrior for battle. Whenever those scenes appear, the poet tends to use more or less the same words and phrases, forming fairly stable blocks of poetry that can be customized as needed to fit their changing contexts. These set pieces, which Lord called *themes*, have much the same function as the verbal formulae—and they, too, slowly form a common stockpile shared by generations of singers. In performance, all this creative activity, this brilliantly choreographed dance of tradition and improvisation, takes place from moment to moment in real time without any reference to a written text.

Epic singers and oral tradition

The Parry–Lord theory sent shockwaves through many scholarly fields. Researchers scoured the surviving texts of early poetry from across Eurasia—the Old Norse *Poetic Edda*, the Old French *chansons de geste*, the Sanskrit epics of India, portions of the Hebrew Bible—for telltale signs of oral composition. Fieldworkers gathered a wealth of unwritten epics, sagas, and folktales preserved in oral traditions all over the world, in the Caucasus, Siberia, Mongolia and Tibet, Japan and Indonesia, large areas of India, and northern and Central Africa. Certain aspects of the oral-formulaic thesis were reworked and refined. Scholars have learned that some cultures prefer different models of oral composition or memorization; every oral tradition follows its own evolutionary path.

Nonetheless, the arts of the poet-singer have much in common across cultures. As a rule, the style of oral epic has a ceremonial flair, rising above common speech, like a national anthem or a wedding vow. Yet it is also marked by immediacy and vigour, sustaining the excitement of a live audience. Some traditional epics are composed in prose, or in a mixture of prose and verse that specialists call *prosimetrum*. Many cultures prefer verse epics, ordered by formal patterns of rhythm and metre, rhyme schemes, alliteration and assonance, and other techniques. The performer's words, whether spoken or sung, are verbal music, often taking the form of rhythmic chanting or a simple repeated melody. Complex melodic patterns are rare and unnecessary. Epic songs are typically accompanied by a musical instrument; these sometimes come from the percussion family, but more popular are stringed instruments resembling a lute or harp, such as the *phorminx* or *kithara* in Homeric Greece, the *balalaika* in parts of Russia, the *dombira* in Central Asia, and the *nkoni* among the Mande peoples of West Africa. This instrumental accompaniment also tends to be simple and repetitive, forming itself around the words.

Oral storytellers love repetition. Their epics abound with parallelism, symmetry, and antithesis. A favourite technique is *parataxis*. This is a method of placing words, phrases, or story elements side by side, in additive fashion, like beads on a string, rather than arranging them into a network of logical relationships, like the atoms in a molecule. This passage from the *Kambili* epic of Mali, performed by Seydou Camara in 1968, artfully uses parataxis and other schemes of repetition to describe a lion man's attacks on the town of Jimini:

> Ah! The Jimini man-eating lion was really playing in Jimini.
>> The lion was going to eat the whole army.
>> He had already finished the water carriers.
>> He had finished the best of the farmers.
>> The lion had finished the horsemen.
>> The lion had finished the learned holy men.
>> The lion had finished the king's children.
>> Ah! It was an awful situation in Jimini.
> The voice of death was in Jimini.

Structures like these are both mnemonic devices for the performer and audience-friendly listening aids. The oral poet's instinct for parallelism can also create rich thematic patterns. A famous example is the mounting tension and drama orchestrated by a parallel series of battle deaths in the last nine books of the *Iliad*, as Zeus' son Sarpedon is killed by Patroclus, then Patroclus by Hector, and finally Hector by Achilles.

Another form of repetition that is widely used in oral epic is *ring composition*, sometimes called *chiastic* design. This is a strategy of repeating words, phrases, or plot episodes in a pattern of concentric rings (ABCBA). Each component has its symmetrical mirror image later in the story, often with small but important variations. Sometimes these designs span only a few verses. Elsewhere, they can form vast tectonic units that extend across an entire epic. Endings have a way of returning to beginnings in this oral world of rings and cycles, where the new and strange is never wholly untethered from what has come before.

All these strategies can produce oral epics that are far longer than the South Slavic songs gathered by Parry and Lord. Recordings of the *Sirat Banī Hilāl* story cycle performed in Egypt and Tunisia, tracing an Arabic tribe's 11th-century migration from the Arabian

Peninsula into North Africa, have ranged from 20 to 32 hours in length. The *Aṇṇanmaar* epic, recited by the Tamil singer E. C. Raamacaami over nineteen summer evenings in 1965, filled 44 hours of audio tape. A version of the *Manas* epic performed in 1979 by a Kyrgyz *manaschi*, Jüsüp Mamay, exceeded 234,000 lines. Even more stunning is a series of performances of *Manas* by Sayaqbay Qaralaev, transcribed in the 1930s and 1940s, that totaled 500,553 verses—almost twenty times longer than the *Iliad* and *Odyssey* combined.

Why are these stories so long? Oral epics are not just old tales; they are storage systems. As they are told and retold, they absorb the knowledge that their cultures deem worth remembering. In communities without writing, epics serve as living archives, preserving information about how the world works, what is known and valued, how things are to be done. For example, in Central Asia, the homeland of Kyrgyz, Uzbek, Kazakh, Turkmen, and other Turkic peoples, thrives a rich literary culture of folktales, ballads, and heroic songs. At the heart of the Kyrgyz oral tradition is the *Manas* epic cycle. Soviet fieldworkers gave the name *manaschi* to the region's celebrated epic singers, both male and female, who told how the legendary hero Manas and his descendants united the forty nomadic Kyrgyz tribes and carved out their historic homeland. The stories seem to have circulated at least since the early 16th century, but they are probably rooted in far older conflicts between the Kyrgyz and their neighbours. The epic songs of the manaschis are giant depositories of knowledge, portraying their people's traditional way of life with encyclopaedic breadth: their history, laws, customs, diet, social arrangements, moral codes, mythology, and cosmology; their interactions with other ethnic groups; their distinctive blending of Islam with older shamanic beliefs and practices; and countless details about the natural and human geography of the Central Asian steppes.

Although oral epics safeguard the past, they do change over time. Oral traditions are sometimes called *homeostatic*. Since they rely on the limited resources of human memory, they maintain a sort of metabolic steady state by continually soaking up new information and discarding older knowledge that no longer serves the community's needs. If a ruling dynasty falls from power, their ancestors might vanish from the old songs. A singer might quietly alter the past to keep pace with changing religious beliefs or the rise of new technologies. Around the year 1900, György Almásy, a foreign collector of *Manas* tales, noticed that the Kyrgyz bards now gave binoculars, revolvers, and other modern inventions to their heroes of long ago. In this way, traditional oral epics will always be unfinished, always co-evolving with the communities that make them.

Most importantly, an oral epic performance is a social event. It is history seen and heard through the singer's performing body. Performances can feature elaborate costumes or symbolic props, acting, dance, ritual, and audience participation. Among the Nyanga people in the Democratic Republic of the Congo, for example, bards who perform epic narratives called *kárisi* often wear special garments and may carry a ceremonial object, such as the conga sceptre associated with the hero of their *Mwindo* epic. The bard accompanies his song with a calabash rattle. After singing each episode, he breaks off the narrative and acts out events from the story, as if playing the role of its hero. Three or four young men, the bard's apprentices, take part in the recital by beating a percussion stick, singing refrains, and voicing praise and encouragement for the singer. The old tales renew themselves with each performance as the storyteller adds or omits materials, or shifts the tone or point of view, to match the audience's mood. For their part, the listeners might hum along, clap their hands, call out praises, and render gifts to the singer, forming a magic circle of shared myths and memories.

The voice in the book

Some decades ago, it was fashionable to distinguish between *primary* (oral) and *secondary* (written) epic. Primary epics came

The singer and the song

from traditional societies without alphabetical literacy. Secondary epics were made for readers in advanced literate cultures. But those labels, too easily warped into false hierarchies of primitive and civilized art, have lately fallen out of use. Scholars have come to realize that orality and literacy are very hard to disentangle. Unwritten traditions can persist long after a society acquires reading and writing. Meanwhile, epics composed in writing can mimic the style of oral poetry. In the Renaissance era, for instance, the great chivalric epics of Matteo Maria Boiardo and Ludovico Ariosto were inspired by Virgil, Dante, and Arthurian romance, but also by hugely popular *cantari cavallereschi*, swashbuckling adventure poems sung by itinerant storytellers in the streets of northern Italy. In Europe's thriving new marketplace of print publication, editions of Ariosto's *Orlando Furioso* (1516–32) ran into the dozens. The poem was issued in monumental folios, festooned with learned prefaces, glosses, and paratexts usually reserved for the work of classical authors. But it was rumoured that Ariosto had plucked some of his stanzas directly from the songs of the travelling *cantastorie*—and, ironically, his *Furioso* was promptly absorbed back into their oral repertoire, which soon swelled with pastiches, adaptations, and parodies of Ariosto's epic.

A key question for today's scholars is how oral epics are altered when they make the journey from voice to text. How fully can we reconstruct lost oral traditions based on the writings they have left behind? Consider *Beowulf*, an Anglo-Saxon heroic poem that survives in a single 11th-century manuscript in the British Library. Its 3,182 lines follow the adventures of a strongman who protects the warrior clans of medieval Scandinavia against the monsters that prey on them. From its enigmatic opening word, 'Hwaet' (variously translated as 'listen', 'hark', 'behold', 'what ho', 'so', or 'bro!'), the poem seems to evoke a lost oral community. Its formulaic diction, its anachronistic hints of social practices dating back to the 6th or 7th century CE, its loving portrayal of bards reciting heroic lays in the firelight of the mead hall—all these clues suggest that the stories told in *Beowulf* evolved for generations in the oral cultures of the early Middle Ages. But the men who finally committed the poem to writing may also have changed its nature. Although Germanic peoples had long used runic alphabets, their vernacular literature was not written down until the coming of Christianity to northern Europe. The missionaries brought with them not only a new writing system but also the literary and religious culture of Latin Christendom. Those who first wield literacy in a society are often members of a priestly or administrative class whose monopoly over written texts is a tool of their social authority. Their elite agendas can profoundly transform the oral traditions they choose to record in writing.

The anonymous *Beowulf*, first set in ink during the 8th to 10th centuries, is a meeting place for the two cultures: oral and literate, popular and priestly. The poet seems to have been acquainted with the Bible, some patristic writings, and maybe even Virgil's *Aeneid*. Glimpses of a Christian worldview flicker across the poem's dark northern landscape. The monster Grendel and other creatures from Germanic folklore are given a biblical heritage:

> the Creator had condemned him
> as one of the seed of Cain—the Everlasting Lord
> avenged Abel's murder. Cain had
> no satisfaction from that feud, but the Creator
> sent him into exile, far from mankind,
> because of his crime. . . .
> In him all evil-doers find their origin,
> monsters and elves and spiteful spirits of the dead,
> also the giants who grappled with God
> for a long while; the Lord gave them their deserts.

Beowulf credits his great exploits in battle to God's favour and protection, and some readers have viewed the hero as an allegorical Christian everyman or even a Christ figure. Yet Beowulf and his Danish allies frequently stray from Christian moral teachings. The poet bluntly declares that the Danes are pagan idol worshippers who suffer because they do not know the true God. The whole poem aches with a gloomy nihilism, a deep sense of the fleeting grandeur of human existence. There is no clear sense of a spiritual afterlife.

We can only guess how this strange amalgam came into being. Scholars have long suspected that a pious Anglo-Saxon monk injected Christian elements into an early manuscript of *Beowulf* to make the pagan poem conform to his religious ideology. But many now believe that no priestly scribe needed to Christianize *Beowulf*. The influence of Christian Latinity could have flowed straight into the oral society of early medieval Britain, maybe through Old English writings that helped to domesticate the foreign traditions of Greece and Rome. Then again, what if *Beowulf* was never an oral epic at all? Could it have been the work of a literate author trying to imitate the style of oral poetry? Many of the poem's celebrated *kennings*—its image-rich compound phrases that often substitute for concrete nouns, such as *hronrād* (whale-road, the sea) or *bānhūs* (bone-house, the human body)—are found in other Anglo-Saxon poems as well, suggesting that they came from a common stock of oral formulae. But roughly half the kennings in *Beowulf*, several hundred altogether, appear nowhere else in the surviving Old English archive. Some readers insist that a poem of such originality, craft, and scope could only have been composed by an author who could read and write.

We find similar tensions between old and new, oral and literate, violence and the sacred, in the great Indian *Mahābhārata*, which probably began to take shape as a story cycle in the oral traditions of South Asia during the late Vedic period (*c.*1100–500 BCE). The oldest portions of the Sanskrit text can be dated to the 5th or 4th century BCE, but the *Mahābhārata* did not reach its final written form until the 5th century CE. Its ancient core was a bardic war epic about a power struggle between two sets of cousins, the Pāṇḍavas and Kauravas, for the kingdom of Hastinapur in northern India. Over time, its prickly warrior ethos was softened by Brahmin elites who wrapped its martial plot in thick layers of folktales, social and political doctrines, philosophical wisdom, and religious allegory. Nearly a thousand years of revision and expansion transformed the old heroic tales into a huge, intricate, polyphonic, sacred epic of Hinduism.

Voice and text, war and faith clash in a different way in the epic poetry of medieval Persia. Abolqasem Ferdowsi's *Shahnameh* (*c.*1010 CE), a legendary chronicle of Iran's heroic past, gathers and reworks a vast corpus of pre-Islamic storytelling to accord with the dominant ideology of Muslim Persia. Ferdowsi's great poem draws on a wide assortment of local oral traditions and historical records derived from Middle Iranian sources. But Ferdowsi was not a cleric going to war with the pagan past; he was a courtly poet who enjoyed the patronage of the wealthy and cosmopolitan Samanid dynasty. When their regime crumbled, he found himself completing his epic under the Turkic Ghaznavids, whose priestly *ulama* class brought with them a narrower, more militant religious orthodoxy. Ferdowsi's epic treads an eclectic path between his Zoroastrian intellectual heritage, the oral legends and lore of ancient Persia, and a muscular Islamic cultural regime that had begun to supplant both. All these poems are caught between worlds, severed from their ancient networks of songcraft but not yet fully at home in our modern climate of reading.

From singer to narrator

The arts of oral performance have slowly faded from memory, eclipsed by the rise of the book. The spread of literacy has spawned a new breed of epics composed in writing for an audience of silent readers. Yet the figure of the epic singer still haunts their pages, as if they yearn to recover the communal intimacy of oral storytelling in earlier times. A striking feature of Western literary epics is the growing prominence of the narrator, as if to fill the void left behind by the absent bard. Ariosto's early critics grumbled over the flamboyant narrator of his *Orlando Furioso*, a smiling rogue who plaits together the poem's many plots, admires his own handiwork, and expresses mock concern for the fates of his fictional creatures. The voice of John Milton's *Paradise Lost* (1667) is transparently the poet himself in old age, blind, persecuted, but inspired with sacred song. William Wordsworth toiled for decades on his autobiographical epic *The Prelude* (1799–1850), a quest to map the contours of his own mind. These were a new breed of poet-hero, striving to preserve the charismatic bond between singer and audience that had been the lifeblood of the oral epic.

The advent of writing also transformed the concept of an epic tradition. An oral epic is traditional because it draws from a common reservoir of heroic legends and, in many cases, a customary lexicon of verbal formulae and themes. But since oral performances are also semi-improvised, every telling is a unique experience that lives for an hour and is gone. An epic composed in writing, by contrast, is a fixed artifact, built to last. A writerly epic tradition therefore becomes a library of classic texts, hallowed and inert, to be pored over, annotated, cross-indexed, and painstakingly copied by authors who seek membership in the tradition. This new world of books spawned a distinct kind of creative imitation. It is known as literary *allusion*: the subtle art of making reference to a word, phrase, idea, character, plot event, or some other element of a prior text, in hopes of calling forth its memory in the reader's mind.

Literary allusions ask us to read the book in our hands as a palimpsest of many texts. Old stories lurk behind new ones like phantoms stalking the living. This has happened before, they whisper; remember us. An allusion calls forth the author's ancestors both to honour and to challenge their legacy, to pay homage to their tradition and to make it their own. One especially rich site of allusion in the Western epic tradition is the Homeric simile. Figures of comparison are common in oral epics. Epic singers often pile up clusters of similes and metaphors to paint vivid word pictures, as when Dirse Kahn tenderly greets his wife in the Turkic *Book of Dede Korkut*:

> Will you come here, my love, the crown of my home?
> Walking along so tall, like a cypress tree,
> With long black hair that falls to her feet,
> With brows like a tightened bow;
> With a mouth too small for two almonds;
> Her red cheeks like the apples of autumn.
> My melon, my lady, my love!

Similes in the Homeric epics are different. Many of them linger over a single image, which swells and exfoliates like an exotic flower. No longer tied to the initial point of comparison, the image starts to attain a rich story life of its own. Homer's *Iliad* compares Achilles' shield to the moon, and then to the flare of a watchfire:

> he lifted up the great, massive
> shield, whose far-reaching gleam was like the moon's.
> As when the gleam of a burning fire appears to sailors
> on the open sea, blazing in a lonely sheepfold, high on
> some mountain, while they are being driven helplessly
> by storms over the fish-rich sea, far from those they love;
> so the gleam from Achilles' splendid, intricately worked
> shield rose up into the clear sky.

The watchfire simile conveys the shield's radiance as it flashes in the sunlight. But more than that, it poignantly evokes a world far from the barren plains of Troy: a realm of natural beauty and human fellowship, of peaceful sheepfolds and warm fires, of loved ones left behind who yearn for their menfolk to come home again. These comparisons thicken the texture of Homer's poetry and widen its scope, drawing the whole human experience into its embrace.

The Homeric simile—utterly distinctive, yet endlessly adaptable—soon became a mainstay of the European epic tradition. Here was a playground for literary allusion, an arena where poets could strive to imitate and outdo their ancestors. In Milton's *Paradise Lost*, it is Satan's shield that resembles the moon:

> his ponderous shield
> Ethereal temper, massy, large, and round,
> Behind him cast; the broad circumference
> Hung on his shoulders like the moon, whose orb
> Through optic glass the Tuscan artist views
> At evening from the top of Fesole,
> Or in Valdarno, to descry new lands,
> Rivers or mountains in her spotty globe.

Milton portrays Satan as a prehistoric prototype of the dazzling warrior Achilles. However, in the Christian poet's reworking of Homer, this Ur-Achilles is a moral monster, warring against a creator god who is the source of all life—and indicting an epic tradition that glorifies violence. But someone else is here too. The 'Tuscan artist' who gazes at the moon through a telescope is the Italian astronomer Galileo. Why has Milton put him here? Is the scientist a symbol of satanic pride? Or does he enjoy privileged access to the secrets of the universe, much like the blind but divinely inspired poet? Or is he rather a model for the poem's readers, who find themselves gazing at the glamorous fallen angel and wondering whether he, like the faraway moon, is truly what he seems? Such are the complex webs of meaning spun by literary allusion, binding new texts to old ones with subtle filaments of likeness and contrast, reverence and rivalry.

Today, the arts of oral-traditional performance are ebbing away, left behind by our globalized, text-centred information age. And yet, over the last century, the rise of modern sound recording and digital media technology, coupled with growing scholarly efforts to document oral cultures around the world, has made our unwritten cultural inheritance more visible and more valuable than ever. For all its rich diversity, worldwide epic literature still draws its unique appeal not only from the memorable deeds of its heroes but also from the lingering presence of the singer in the song.

Chapter 3
The epic hero

An epic is the story of a hero. Standing in the spotlight, in the eye of the storm, the hero is the epic's brilliant focal point. Epics express humanity's desire to leave our mark on the universe, to be seen and remembered. In their drive to change the world, epic heroes face ordeals that push them to the extreme boundaries of human existence. Whether they succeed or fail, whether they embody our ideals or defy them, they inspire our awe. Epic heroes walk alone as individuals touched by greatness. They experience life with a special intensity. In their struggles against adversity, they test the limits of human possibility.

The world's epic heroes are no less diverse than the cultures that created them. But they do share some family resemblances. Heroic literature is concerned with extraordinary striving and suffering. Epic heroes have rare talents that set them apart from other human beings. They are exceptional creatures, one of a kind. In today's media, we see everyday people rising to heroism in moments of crisis, often through praiseworthy acts of courage and self-sacrifice. They rescue neighbors from burning buildings, thwart crimes in progress, donate organs to strangers. The greatness of the traditional epic hero is different. It is an inborn disposition, burning to manifest itself in a life of purposeful action. Epic heroes are spiritual aristocrats. They typically spring from an elite social class and enjoy unusual gifts of body or mind. Many traits can distinguish these heroes—strength, endurance, cunning—but they share a powerful force of will. They feel driven to exert control over a world that resists their prerogatives, to stamp their names on a hostile landscape and make it their own. Their compulsive need to assert their will, to be themselves, captures our imagination and shows us what humanity, at its best and boldest, can do.

Epic heroes are not gods, even though many have divine parentage and nearly all possess special abilities that surpass our own. They are fundamentally human. They eat, sleep, and bleed as we do. They matter to us because they resemble us. The sense of wonder that they inspire has much to do with the ongoing contest between their outsized ambitions and their human limitations. They stumble as often as they soar. They err, misbehave, lose heart, hurt themselves or those they love, and mourn their losses. They live in precarious worlds where achievement is won at the cost of pain and risk. Since, like us, they are subject to death, they pursue their goals with the passionate vigor of mortal beings who have something to fight for and everything to lose. It is their role as heightened versions of ourselves, throbbing with vitality, straining against the fixed boundaries of the human condition, that gives epic heroes their unique charisma and makes their stories endure.

The origins of the hero

The English word *hero*, like its many cognates in other European languages, derives from the Greek *hērōs*. This is a mysterious word of unknown origin. Some have traced its ancestry back to the Proto-Indo-European root **ser-*, to guard, to protect. Or possibly (and unsettlingly?) its root is **séru̯-/*sóru-*, loot, booty. Others would link *hērōs* with Hera, the Greek goddess of marriage, and the figure of a virile young bridegroom. A further theory is that *hērōs* was once a social rank or title, naming a warrior aristocracy in the Mycenaean world. It seems fitting that the word's etymology is so obscure, rising from some deep, untraceable wellspring. For when the Greek epic cycle took shape in the 8th century BCE, the heroes whose stories it told were already consigned to a faraway past. Homer and Hesiod portrayed them as semi-divine beings, often born from the sexual union of a mortal and a god. Many other societies have harbored similar views of a lost heroic age. In those bygone days, their ancestors strove more mightily and shone more brightly than those who came after them. The landmark study by H. M. and N. K. Chadwick, *The Growth of Literature* (1932–40), found this pattern in world cultures from Russia to Polynesia, from the ancient Near East to Celtic Britain. In epic traditions across this vast region, the old glory days are sealed off from the present, remote, intangible, like a dream after waking.

For the Chadwicks, though, the age of heroes was no dream. They believed that many societies had experienced a real-life heroic age, a distinct set of historical conditions that gave birth to the heroes of epic songs. These were times of instability and conflict. Older bonds of kinship had weakened, but modern national identities had not yet been forged. People lived in small communities governed by military aristocracies. Thriving on heroic violence, their warlords strove for dominance in raids, skirmishes, and feuds with rival chieftains. Codes of honour brought some discipline to the battlefield and heaped status on the warriors who most ably served their overlords. The war band—the Romans called it a *comitatus*—was bound together not by family ties but rather by mutual loyalties, obligations, gift exchanges, and, above all, by the precious currency of honour that measured each warrior's public standing in his community. This was human civilization in its hot-headed adolescence: fierce, independent, competitive, hungry for glory. The Chadwicks located these heroic ages at diverse times and places across Afro-Eurasia. They often came in the wake of some great social upheaval, such as the Bronze Age collapse that shook the eastern Mediterranean world in the 12th century BCE, or the *Völkerwanderungzeit*, the tide of Germanic migrations that crashed against the Western Roman Empire in the 4th through 6th centuries CE.

Did all these heroic societies really exist? The archaeological remains are scanty and hard to interpret. But one of the Chadwicks' key insights does ring true: whatever its political organization might be, a warrior elite needed its poets. Court singers likely played an important role in such image-conscious honour cultures. They were the celebrity publicists of their day. As rulers doled out booty to reward their leading magnates, the poets doled out praise. In late antique Europe, for example, Roman geographers told of oral poets living in Britain and Gaul, known by the Celts as *bardoi* (the origin of our term *bard*), who sang the exploits of famous men to the music of the lyre. Epic literature has long enjoyed close ties to this kind of panegyric poetry. Some scholars believe that epic traditions all over the world might have evolved from simple praise songs for burly warlords long ago.

Epic, folktale, and myth

Of course, an epic is not just a round of applause. Praise poetry is static and retrospective; epic heroes are always in motion. Their natural medium is narrative action, not lyric repose. To tell their stories, epics draw from a wider range of ancient narrative forms, including myths and folktales. Odysseus' encounter with the man-eating Cyclops in Homer's *Odyssey*, for instance, has hundreds of parallels in folk narratives from Iceland to Mongolia. All those wily men outwitting one-eyed giants in every corner of Eurasia—this pattern tells us that the Homeric tradition must have absorbed a popular regional folktale into Odysseus' biography. Folk motifs loom even larger in the famous quest of Jason and the Argonauts, a story told in Greco-Roman epics such as Apollonius Rhodius' *Argonautica* (3rd century BCE). A hero comes to a strange land where a menacing sorcerer or ogre dwells. The tyrant imposes a series of impossible tasks on the hero, such as taming wild beasts or sowing and harvesting a field in a single day. The hero performs those tasks with help from his oppressor's daughter, who has fallen in love with him. They flee, and the daughter uses her magical powers to thwart their pursuers.

Versions of this popular story can be found all over the world, from the ancient Sumerians to modern-day Tibet.

These interactions between epic traditions and folktales can stretch and twist the fibres of the epic hero's identity. As a rule, the heroes of folktales are nameless everymen. Rarely of high birth, they are ordinary people who find themselves in extraordinary situations. Their inner lives are a blank. Showing little individuality or force of will, they drift from one encounter to the next in a mysterious world beyond their control. None of those traits befits the epic hero, that headstrong, singular personality whose name means everything. To weave folktale episodes into heroic epics is to draw these opposing forces into a creative tension. Epic heroes might sometimes surprise us by shrinking from a fight or stooping to guile and skullduggery. Jason steals the golden fleece by night, relying on Medea's potion to put its dragon guardian to sleep. Odysseus sneakily escapes the Cyclops' cave by strapping himself to the belly of a sheep.

Mythology and religion also colour the epic hero's identity. Storytelling traditions that stretch from the Caucasus to Southeast Asia are especially rich in heroes who straddle the boundary between the human and divine realms. In parts of northern Asia, epic tales and sagas portray culture heroes who look very much like primeval creator gods. The Yakut hero Er-Sogotokh is the ancestral parent of the human race. An orphan hero (his name means solitary man), he endures great ordeals to find a wife and become the forebear of the Yakut peoples. In other traditions, such as the enormous *Gesar* epic cycle from Mongolia and Tibet, the heroes are gods who take on human flesh to rid the earth of demonic forces. They are objects of ritual devotion, and their epics are sometimes recited at religious festivals in their honour. Arjuna and his four Pāṇḍava brothers, the heroes of the Indic *Mahābhārata*, are also semi-divine beings, bearing the attributes of their father gods. Local cults of Pāṇḍava worship still flourish across India today. In the poem's famous sixth book, known as the

Bhagavad Gītā, Arjuna's friend and charioteer Krishna reveals himself in all his glory as an incarnation of the god Viṣṇu. Epic traditions in Africa move even more easily between the human and spirit worlds. These stories are tightly enmeshed with other cultural practices such as divination, sacrifice, and spiritual healing that enfold human life within a sacred cosmos.

In the West, by contrast, the epic hero has walked a long, winding path of secularization. Some scholars believe that epic traditions have a natural tendency to demythologize old beliefs. Over long periods of time, their stories slowly but surely transform gods and demons into merely human heroes. Northern European heroic songs about the dragon slayer Sigurd or Siegfried, for example, might have evolved from older myths about the gods Thor and Baldr. In Homer's heroes, too, we glimpse the remnants of ancient Near Eastern myths about clashing gods and demigods. But the warriors who shed their blood at Troy are only human:

> As is the family of leaves, so it is also with men:
> the wind scatters the leaves on the ground, but the forest breaks
> into bud and makes more when the spring season comes round.
> So with the family of men, one generation grows and another ceases.

Mortality is the bitter inheritance that divides the Western epic hero from the deathless gods. Still, the divine aura has not quite gone dark in these mighty men. As the Homeric poems coalesced in the 8th century BCE, they formed bonds with local hero cults that flourished across the Greek-speaking world. The hero cults blended the new civic identities of the nascent Greek city states with ancient practices of ancestor worship. Like Homer's warriors, the cult heroes were mortal beings, their deaths honoured with ritual mourning at annual festivals. Yet they also received sacrificial offerings as living avatars and protectors of their communities. Similar forms of ancestor worship seem to have thrived among the Egyptians and other Near Eastern societies. We still have much to learn about the relationship between the Greek hero cults and the Homeric epics. It seems clear, at least, that the sacred tombs of those ancient heroes, symbolizing their mortality but also marking their ongoing role in the civic life of their people, share a powerful kinship with the epic tradition, which calls on its heroes to burn brightly, die gloriously, and live forever in public memory.

A universal hero?

The epic's close ties to other cultural traditions—panegyric, folktale, myth, and cult—help to explain why epic heroes from far-flung regions have so much in common. In all these forms, their stories must have flowed along the vast trade arteries that linked merchants, diplomats, soldiers, priests, mercenaries, and migrants all over the ancient world. But could the true source of those resemblances lie elsewhere? Might it lodge inside each of us? Inspired by the psychoanalytic thought of Sigmund Freud and Carl Jung, some students of comparative mythology believe that heroic tales around the globe share the same basic templates, often called *archetypes*, that are inborn and universal, the unconscious birthright of all human beings. In his influential book *The Hero with a Thousand Faces* (1949), Joseph Campbell gathered many of those heroic tropes into a single master plot that he called the *monomyth*: a blueprint of the hero's journey that underwrites many epics, legends, and myths worldwide. For Campbell, the monomyth is so enduring because, properly understood, the hero's journey is also our own. It is a pattern for every human life, a symbolic reflection of our everyday quest for spiritual enlightenment.

Campbell's seventeen-part framework begins with the hero's call to adventure, typically a quest that leads the hero into an unknown realm of wonders. Guided by a mystical guardian and equipped with magical weapons or talismans, the hero reluctantly crosses the threshold into this dangerous new world. A series of initiatory trials ensues. Supernatural beings confront the hero, often through erotic temptations or through symbolic projections of parental authority. The hero might travel to an underworld or experience death or dismemberment. At last, the hero attains the quest object. Further challenges mark the journey back to the realm of everyday life, where the hero's hard-won wisdom can be shared with the community. Although the world's great storytelling traditions rarely include all those elements, Campbell reads them as fragmentary versions of the same master plot, all conveying the same fundamental truth: the hero's quest is both a physical ordeal and a psychological journey, guiding us toward self-discovery and inner transformation.

Campbell's method is brilliant and flawed. Critics point out that many traditional stories do not fit his schema. Some have asked whether his monomyth has a Western cultural bias, shoehorning the world's literary forms into a European psychoanalytic model of human selfhood. In fact, epic traditions have long attracted archetype hunters. Before Campbell, cultural anthropologists such as Edward Burnett Tylor and FitzRoy Richard Somerset Raglan had proposed sweeping theories of myth and ritual to explain worldwide hero patterns. We can trace this kind of thinking all the way back to the 6th century BCE, when the ancient Greeks sifted through Homer's epics in search of hidden allegorical wisdom. Following their lead, the Stoic and Neoplatonic philosophers of late antiquity inspired generations of medieval Christians to read Virgil's *Aeneid* as a moral allegory, its hero's adventures teaching everyday lessons for a good life. Literary criticism loves to pluck universal truths from the clutter of particularity. But hero-pattern scholars can too easily lose sight of what makes each story unique. How much can Campbell teach us about the epic hero, we might ask, when his monomyth applies just as well to Hercules, the Buddha, and Harry Potter?

Let us try narrowing our field of view. If we focus on the heroes of traditional oral epics, in all their endless variety, we do find some striking commonalities. Whether they hail from Central Africa, western Ireland, or the Russian steppes, many of them have similar life stories. For Western readers who expect epic poems to begin *in medias res*, it might come as a surprise that the world's folk epics usually narrate the hero's life story in chronological order, from cradle to grave. What does this heroic biography look like?

The traditional epic hero's origins tend to be mysterious or unnatural. Typically fathered by an animal or a god, these special men and women bestride the domains of nature and the supernatural, time and eternity. Since their status as heroes is inborn, their stories often linger over their gestation, birth, and early childhood. They may be born to elderly or barren parents, like the Uzbek hero Alpamyš, or by caesarian section, like Rostam in Ferdowsi's *Shahnameh*, or through incest, like Sinfjötli in the *Völsungasaga*. Their strange birth might be foretold by prophecies or marked by omens. In a version of the Banyanga *Mwindo* epic, the hero performs household chores for his mother while he is still in her womb, and he is born by passing through her middle finger. In the oldest extant birth narrative of the Irish hero Cú Chulainn, his mother, Deichtine, daughter of the king of Ulster, conceives the child by the god Lugh, aborts him so that she may marry her betrothed, but then, as a new bride, becomes pregnant with Cú Chulainn once again and bears him as her son. Since the circumstances of the epic hero's birth are so odd, they portend a singular personhood and a manifest destiny. But they also affirm that the hero, born of woman, belongs to humankind.

As children, epic heroes quickly reveal their unusual nature. They are often naughty and quarrelsome. Their early maturation is either very fast or very slow. Many show prodigious strength or endurance at a young age. They might start speaking as soon as they are born, like Mwindo, or slay wild animals during their infancy, like the Armenian hero David of Sassoun. Overleaping the normal stages of human development, they hurtle toward adulthood as their special nature yearns to express itself in glorious action. Others do not speak or walk until they reach some hidden milestone that activates their heroic potential. The Kyrgyz hero Manas is a mischievous boy who appears slow-witted and begins walking at the age of 5, his true identity kept secret until he reaches adolescence and sets out to destroy his people's oppressors. Sunjata (also called Son-Jara or Sundiata), the legendary founder of the Mali Empire, is lame for much of his boyhood due to the sorcery of his father's jealous co-wives. These examples also show that the young hero's ties to kith and kin can be tenuous. Some epic heroes are foundlings; others spend their early lives in hiding or in exile. In due time, their stories will often bring them home again, as either ally or enemy, to shore up an identity that their families left unformed in childhood.

Set apart from their communities, these heroes walk alone on the road of adventure. They are essentially lonely beings, even if they are accompanied by helpers or companions in arms. Their unique character cannot fully express itself in civilized society. Sometimes they touch the outer edges of human nature. The transformation of humans into animals, a beloved theme in world mythology, is common in the epic traditions of Celtic Europe, in Northeast Asia, and throughout Africa. Even in heroic tales that do not portray such wonders, we sometimes still see the faint imprint of tooth and claw. In the *Táin Bó Cuailnge*, for example, the hero earns his nickname (Cú Chulainn, the Hound of Culann) after he kills the vicious watchdog of Culann the smith, who is so distraught that the boy vows to serve him in the dog's place. Anglo-Saxonists, meanwhile, have long suspected that *Beowulf* owes something to the Bear's Son folktales found across Eurasia—stories about a monster-slaying strongman who was begotten or reared by bears—even if some scholars no longer believe that Beowulf's name comes from the Old English epithet 'bee-wolf' (i.e. bear, enemy of bees). Many epic heroes bond with animal companions and guardians, such as Gesar's flying horse, Kyang Go Karkar, or the phoenix-like Simorgh who cares for the abandoned infant Zāl in Ferdowsi's *Shahnameh*. Even the poets of the Virgilian epic tradition routinely compare their warring champions to wild animals. All these patterns express the hero's dual role as a community leader and an outsider, harnessed but untamed, in whom civilization and the wilderness strive for dominance.

The hero in society

In our age of the novel, we might expect the socially isolated epic hero to be a brooding, introspective soul. But the epic is no place for a Raskolnikov or a Jane Eyre. Epic heroes are public figures. Their selfhood faces outward rather than inward. They act upon the world and make it bear witness to their achievements. Instead of peering into their own hidden depths, they see themselves through others' eyes. When meeting a stranger, they boldly recite their curriculum vitae. They cherish the visible symbols of their heroic identity, such as battle trophies and lavish gifts from grateful patrons. They rarely doubt themselves or question their own prerogatives.

All of this makes the epic hero a social problem. Myth and folktale generally take place in fantasy realms, lawless neverlands where the normal rules of human relations do not apply. Epic narratives, by contrast, cluster along the boundary between myth and history. Their heroes, for all their godlike freedom of action, belong to human civilization as we do. They often serve and defend their communities. They might not personally embody all their people's values or norms of conduct—some heroes, such as Mwindo, Krishna, or Jason, serially violate them—but their heroic identities are still tethered to the legal, economic, religious, and political lives of their societies. The epic hero is a paradoxical figure: an outsider, a breed apart, whose personhood depends on the same sticky web of social relations that constrains the hero's independence. Standing aloof from their communities, epic heroes somehow also stand with them and for them.

This uneasy relationship between hero and community often brings the hero into conflict with political authority. In traditional epics, the hero and chieftain may be the same person: Gilgamesh, Manas, Gesar, Sunjata. But more complex societies can pry apart the sovereign's deliberative and executive functions, putting the pen and the sword in different hands. Some epics make the warrior-hero an ally or vassal of the political sovereign. When the ruler is foolish, capricious, or corrupt, the hero must ponder his loyalty to an unworthy regime. In other worldwide epic traditions, the hero is an outlander whose arrival on the scene threatens the established political order. In the extremely popular *Köroğlu* cycle of the Oghuz Turks, an epic tradition now widely shared by the Turkic, Kurdish, Armenian, and Arab peoples of Central Asia, the hero's fluid identity allows him to assume either role, the chieftain or the outsider, to match the local political culture. The legendary Köroğlu (also known as Görogly or Gurughli) is apparently based on a real-life 16th-century bandit. In the northern regions of Central Asia, where nomadic pastoralists clashed for centuries in intertribal conflicts, he is portrayed as an elite, high-born governor of a Turkmen tribe who defends their ancestral homeland against the Arabs and other ethnic rivals. In more settled and sedentary cultures further south, Köroğlu came to be viewed as a Robin Hood figure, an outlaw whose band of common labourers fought back against the greed and injustice of the Ottoman aristocracy.

The tensions between hero and king are often more subtle: a problem of structure, we might say, more than of politics. For the epic hero is usually a wanderer at heart, a freelance, who makes an uneasy compact with political authority. While the king sits and administers, the hero is on the move. Rulers watch over the welfare of their subjects and the territorial integrity of their domains. The hero's purpose is to reap the full measure of his or her unique potential for greatness. Many of the world's epics explore what happens when those goals fall out of alignment. This is the spark that ignites so much pain and death in Homer's *Iliad*, for example, when the Achaeans' best warrior, Achilles, walks off the Trojan battlefield in response to a personal slight from his commander in chief.

In medieval Europe, feudal epics like the *Chanson de Roland* (*c.*1100 CE) took a keen interest in the power relations that bind the knight to the institutional authority of church and crown. In the poem, Charlemagne longs for a united, militant Christendom, but his court is a snake pit of bickering political factions. The epic's climax comes when the Christian warrior Roland is ambushed by Saracen hordes in the Pyrenees. Although his troops are badly outnumbered, Roland refuses to summon Charlemagne's reinforcements by blowing his oliphaunt horn until it is too late. Many scholars now deplore Roland's failure to call for help as a sign of tragic overconfidence or pride. The poem, however, treats his death as an inspiring act of martyrdom. The hero's fanatical charisma far outshines Charlemagne's grim and enfeebled bureaucracy. For centuries, Roland's descendants wandered through the pages of chivalric epics and romances, forcing their authors to weigh the competing claims of the one and the many, unity and diversity, discipline and freedom. And no wonder, since their stories mirrored a real-life power struggle between Western Europe's wealthy, independent-minded feudal aristocracies and its ascendant royal houses. Roland's last bedraggled offspring was to be Don Quixote, the hapless knight errant of Cervantes' 1605 novel, whose stubborn refusal to obey any man's law but his own reaches its natural conclusion in madness.

A rarer form of heroic freedom from social constraints is the female epic hero. Conservative social and religious mores tend to constrict the roles of women in traditional epic storytelling. They are supporters, allies, enemies, but seldom protagonists with starring roles in their own adventures. There are rich exceptions, of course. In some cases, religious communities have carved out special zones in the landscape of world epic where women may heroically defend their faith or become objects of worship themselves. In the fragmentary Old English *Judith*, for example, found in the same 10th-century manuscript as *Beowulf*, the Hebraic heroine beheads the villainous general Holofernes and musters an army to rout his Assyrian forces—a rallying cry, perhaps, for beleaguered Anglo-Saxons who had endured decades of Viking invasions.

A more recent discovery is the *Epic of Siri*, recited for fieldworkers in the early 1990s by the Tulu singer Gopala Naika in India's Karnataka province. The story describes Siri's miraculous birth, her conflicts with her husband and his male community, her exile and remarriage, her posthumous divinity, and the family troubles that burden her daughters and granddaughters. More than 15,000 verses in length, the epic is performed at religious ceremonies in which female worshipers are possessed by the spirits of Siri and other women in the poem. Enmeshed in a living ecology of cultic practices devoted to a female deity, the epic has been able to maintain its independence from other south Indian storytelling traditions that focus on the lives of violent men. Much more shall be said of warrior maidens and other heroines in later chapters.

The hero looks inward

Epic heroes chafe against laws that curb their freedom. In complex societies, however, our institutions do not simply force norms of conduct upon us. We internalize those norms. Church and state whisper to us with the inner voice of piety or conscience. In the Western epic canon, when the hero's free will clashes with a higher authority, the result is often self-division and inner conflict. Many of Europe's epic heroes learned that lesson from Virgil's Aeneas, who struggles not just to defeat his foreign enemies but also to stifle his own desires and let the gods have their way with him. Since the late Middle Ages, the Western epic tradition has slowly and tentatively mapped the terrain of this new battleground, the hero's own wayward heart. One of its keenest explorers is Milton's Satan in *Paradise Lost*. The fallen angel stares with horror into the gulf between his angelic past and the fallen creature he has become:

> Me miserable! Which way shall I fly
> Infinite wrath, and infinite despair?
> Which way I fly is hell; myself am hell;
> And in the lowest deep a lower deep
> Still threatening to devour me opens wide,
> To which the hell I suffer seems a heaven.

Himself a rebel who had cheered on the execution of King Charles I in 1649, Milton had suffered the crushing defeat of his own political ideals when the English Commonwealth collapsed a decade later. Like Virgil's Aeneas, Milton's Satan is a victim of war, a wandering refugee who dreams of planting the flag of empire on a faraway shore. Yet he cannot escape his own private hell of remorse and shame (see Figure 2). Satan is not just a chest-beating *miles gloriosus*, senselessly smashing himself against divine omnipotence. He has the psychological complexity of a failed revolutionary. Routed on the battlefield, he now wages an endless war within himself, assailed at once by wounded vanity, defiance, and despair.

The rebel-heroes of the Romantic era owe much to Milton's Satan. The Romantic poets' experiments in literary epic, like Milton's, were shaped by revolutionary fervour and disappointment. 'I want a hero,' writes Lord Byron at the outset of his mock-heroic masterpiece *Don Juan* (1824). True heroism, he complains, can scarcely be found in his unworthy era. In the gloomy aftermath of the French Revolution, many would-be epic poets turned inward. They hoped that by probing the roots of human selfhood, they might revive the ideals of liberty and justice that had been stifled by 19th-century Europe's reactionary politics. Soaring philosophical poems such as William Blake's *Jerusalem* (1820) and Percy Bysshe

2. Satan lamenting his fall, an engraving by John Baptist Medina
for the 1688 edition of Milton's *Paradise Lost*.

Shelley's *Prometheus Unbound* (1820) blame the shallow conformity and materialism of their age for crushing the human spirit. Yet their protagonists also suffer from self-doubt and disillusionment as they struggle to emancipate the imagination, to break the shackles of a godless world, and to find divinity within themselves.

These Promethean rebels voice a growing pessimism, a fear that no one can rise above the deterministic social forces set in motion by the Industrial Revolution. In the age of Adam Smith, Jeremy Bentham, and Karl Marx, the epic hero's charisma withered before the impersonal gods of the marketplace and the machine. Trapped inside the high walls of the poet's own utopian imagination, the inward-looking Romantic hero also reflects a deeper crisis of faith in old epic ideals. Rising from the darkness of ancient myth, epic heroes had once been awe-inspiring supermen. Now they began to look like thuggish egotists or lonesome dreamers, poorly equipped to survive in the glare of modern history. For centuries, the Western epic tradition had grown ever more suspicious of its own hero worship. Some of its heroes must recruit large groups of adventurers, such as Jason's Argonauts, because they are too weak to stand alone. Others misuse their special gifts, like Julius Caesar in Lucan's *De Bello Civili*, whose thirst for power makes his nation bleed. Christian poets struggled for centuries with the ethics of heroic violence: for example, Walter of Châtillon's *Alexandreis* (*c.*1171–81), which rivalled Virgil and Dante in popularity during the High Middle Ages, invites the reader to marvel at Alexander the Great's conquest of Persia and India even as it questions his moral character and casts doubt on his imperial dreams. Still other heroes simply cannot adapt to changing times. In the German *Nibelungenlied*, a traditional epic strongman, Siegfried, is betrayed and murdered by lesser men whose social world is too complex for him to understand.

Stuffing their poems with soul-searching, speechifying titans, the Romantics tried to revive the epic hero but may have only hastened a long decline. To be sure, many 19th-century poets tried to rekindle the glories of yesteryear—whether with earnest idealism, as in Robert Southey's hymn to republican liberty, *Joan of Arc* (1796), or with wistful melancholy, as in Alfred Tennyson's Arthurian cycle, *Idylls of the King* (1859-85). A few poems, such as Elizabeth Barrett Browning's *Aurora Leigh* (1856), argued that a modern age demanded brand new heroes:

> if there's room for poets in this world
> A little overgrown (I think there is),
> Their sole work is to represent the age,
> Their age, not Charlemagne's,—this live, throbbing age,
> That brawls, cheats, maddens, calculates, aspires,
> And spends more passion, more heroic heat,
> Betwixt the mirrors of its drawing-rooms,
> Than Roland with his knights at Roncesvalles.

The dominant feeling, though, was an awkward sense of anachronism, a literary tradition grown old and moribund. Crumpled in the gyres of history, weakened from within by compulsive self-scrutiny, the epic hero was to limp into the 20th century as a shrunken everyman with a dwindling sphere of influence.

A mortal hero

For all their diversity, the world's epic heroes are limited creatures like the rest of us. They are born to strive, suffer, and die. Yet since their unique gifts so far exceed our own, they push more boldly against their human limitations. No limit is more absolute—and therefore more repugnant to the epic hero—than death itself. In fact, the epic hero's attitude toward dying is something of a paradox. These characters have a special intimacy with death. Most of us shun it, but their incandescent energy drives them toward it. Knowing their time is fleeting, they race to fill their lives with meaningful action. They are the volunteers, the expeditionaries, the martyrs. As slayers of men and monsters, epic heroes also carry death in their own hands, wresting their desired goal from a universe that will not yield it up without some cost in blood. Epic heroes often die young, sacrificing themselves for their community or for a lofty principle worth fighting for. When they come to their final hours on the field of human endeavour, their greatness tends to flare up with unusual radiance, as if the coming of death electrifies their short lives with glory in one last defiant reckoning with the infinite.

Yet although these heroes surround themselves with death, they do not desire it. In all their many forms, epic heroes stand for life. They live more fully than we do, more passionately and vibrantly. They long to impose their will on the world. But death does not answer to their demands. Death is the epic hero's natural enemy because it is the supreme constraint on human freedom. The hero's mortality is therefore a thorny issue for epic storytellers. They might choose to push the hero's death outside the frame of the story, as an inevitable but faraway prospect that is better left unspoken. Or the dying hero might achieve or revert to divinity. Or some other kind of eternal reward might await the hero in the afterlife. Such consolations might enable the hero to face the coming of death with self-composure. Leaving behind a legacy in this world might also solace the hero with a sort of life after death—as when the dying Beowulf, gazing on the treasure hoard of the dragon he has slain, takes comfort in the knowledge that he gave his life to provide for his people.

Just as often, epic heroes meet death with wild protest. On a beach near Troy, Achilles tearfully complains to his mother, the sea nymph Thetis, that Agamemnon has taken his rightful war prize from him—a desperate loss because Achilles knows he is fated to die soon, leaving only his glory behind. Beset by Saracens in a mountain pass at Roncevaux, Roland finds himself hopelessly outnumbered but resolves to go down fighting. The dying Siegfried, stabbed in the back while hunting in the Rhineland, lashes out in helpless rage at the cowards who took his life so shamefully. After eating the forbidden fruit of knowledge, Milton's Adam and Eve spend many dark hours lamenting the curse of death they have incurred, a curse which will not take effect at once, but slowly, excruciatingly, so that every human life is now 'a long day's dying to augment our pain'.

Humanity's struggle with mortality lies close to the heart of the Western epic tradition. Many of these poems conclude with mourning for the dead. But death also drives epic heroes to make a lasting impact on their communities. Epic literature expresses a deep human need for creative achievement in the shadow of our own finitude. The hero's war with death began very early in world epic; the battle lines were already drawn 4,000 years ago in the *Epic of Gilgamesh*. The hero scoffs at death until his beloved friend Enkidu becomes mortally ill. He can do nothing as he watches Enkidu's life ebb away. Then, for seven days, Gilgamesh clings in anguish to his friend's decomposing corpse. When a maggot drops from Enkidu's nostril, the hero finally yields him up for burial. Now Gilgamesh truly knows death, and he is terrified. The rest of the poem depicts his gruelling quest for the secret of eternal life—a search that ends in failure. Gilgamesh reaches the mysterious realm of Uta-Napishti (a man who, like the biblical Noah, has survived a universal flood) and obtains a special plant that can make him young again, but a serpent steals it during his journey home. The poem ends with Gilgamesh, empty-handed, pondering his great city of Uruk. He has fortified the city, rebuilt its sturdy walls, made its people safe and prosperous. This will be his legacy: Gilgamesh must die, but these walls will stand for many ages. He has achieved a kind of immortality in their enduring brickwork, and in the epic poem that tells his story.

Epic heroes are overachievers, surpassing all the rest in strength and vigour. But they fascinate us because they resemble us. In their sufferings, triumphs, and failures, if we look hard enough, we can see reflections of our own. In another way, too, epic heroes are like us: they act, build, make, lead, and conquer so that they will be remembered. That is perhaps the deepest message of the world's epic traditions. They show us that through memory, through storytelling, the human will can defy death.

Chapter 4
War

> Sing, goddess, the anger of Achilles, Peleus' son,
> the accursed anger which brought the Achaeans countless
> agonies and hurled many mighty shades of heroes into Hades,
> causing them to become the prey of dogs and
> all kinds of birds; and the plan of Zeus was fulfilled.

The Western epic tradition begins with rage. *Mēnis* (wrath) is the first word in Homer's *Iliad* and its driving theme. This will be a story about the anger that burns within Achilles, the godlike Greek warrior, when his commanding officer dishonours him. But anger spreads like wildfire through the poem. Quarrels flare up among the Olympian gods. Greeks clash with Trojans and bicker with one another. The Trojans seethe with fury at Paris and Helen, whose adultery begot all this pain. Rage takes hold of nearly everyone who witnesses the waste and folly of a war that is now in its 10th year.

Yet without the Trojan War, there would have been no song of Achilles. The rage that will destroy him will also make him live forever. Even though he spends three-quarters of the *Iliad* sulking in his tent, far from the fighting, Achilles cannot withdraw from battle for long because war defines him. He needs it in order to be himself. War is the epic hero's natural element. We have already seen that epic heroes are creatures of supreme energy and volition. When they try to bend the world to their will, they soon find themselves pushing against resistance. As a result, the hero's career is a string of conflicts and confrontations. Only through aggression—and, nearly always, through violence—can the hero change the fundamental order of things.

Blocking the hero's path are bristling ranks of men and monsters who would measure the hero's force of will against their own. The opponents face each other across a battlefield flooded with testosterone, where every ordeal is a public test of manhood. By and large, the traditional epic is an arena of male competition, celebrating the quick temper and the strong arm. Its combatants speak a language well known to the parents of teenage boys: crude insults, locker-room boasts, dominance rituals. Steeped in aggression, the epic has a long history of violence. In his brilliant book *How to Kill a Dragon* (1995), the linguist Calvert Watkins traces a single Indo-European word pattern—HERO SLAY SERPENT—across a vast range of myths and heroic tales from Vedic India to medieval Scandinavia. Watkins argues that this phrase, relentlessly repeated in cognate forms across many languages, must have arisen from an ancient story about a mighty dragon killer. Over time, the formula mutated to include other kinds of heroic bloodletting: HERO SLAY MONSTER; HERO SLAY HERO. This primordial act of violence—a hand raised in anger to kill a foe—has replicated itself for thousands of years, like a genetic blueprint, in the deep structure of heroic poetry from Armenia to Ireland. This might be why the epic has so often found a home in the courts of military elites, where it upholds a tough warrior mentality etched in blood. Hero slays; hero is remembered. When Alexander the Great launched his conquest of the Persian Empire in 334 BCE, according to Plutarch, he brought a copy of Homer's *Iliad* with him. Alexander began his campaign with a visit to the site of Troy, where he made an offering at the legendary tomb of Achilles.

Epics sing of strife and slaughter. Yet no literary form broods more deeply over the consequences of war. The *Iliad* begins with Achilles' wrath. At once we learn its terrible cost: all those souls thrust into darkness, those bodies lying broken on the plains of Troy. The Homeric epics show us war in all its beauty and desolation. In the early years of World War II, the French philosopher Simone Weil wrote a haunting essay entitled 'The *Iliad*, or The Poem of Force' (1940). For Weil, the poem's true concern is not Achilles or Hector but force itself, the awful power wielded by the strong over the weak. Homer shows that force enslaves both the victors and the victims of war. Through the cruel psychology of force, the victors come to view the vanquished as subhuman—and, in losing sight of their victims' humanity, the victors lose their own. Then the tide of battle turns, and the victims now lash out in blind pain to kill their victimizers. On the battlefield, where the threat of death looms everywhere, there can be no empathy, no ethics. There is only the inexorable machinery of force, remorselessly crushing the human soul. Weil's experience of militant fascism in Europe clearly shaped her reading of the *Iliad*. What she saw better than most, however, was how deeply the Homeric poems ponder the psychic toll of violence. They are not alone in this. Epic traditions all over the world dwell on the pain and loss that are the price of heroic action.

A beautiful death

Built for combat, most epic heroes are physically imposing. They are muscular and athletic. Many are prodigiously large. We are invited to admire their bodies and to marvel at their feats of strength. They can hurl massive objects or wield weapons that are too heavy for their puny descendants. Their dominance often extends beyond the battle arena. They excel at elite pastimes such as hunting or athletic games, testing grounds where they can measure their prowess against wild beasts or lesser men. Such are the famous sporting contests and funeral games that give Homer's warriors a periodic recess from battle, or at least a different way to release their competitive energy. It might be no coincidence that the first Olympic games took place in the early 8th century BCE, just as the Homeric epics were taking form.

Some epic heroes are always looking for a fight. Others counsel against it. But as soon as they reach the front lines, they share the easy self-assurance of a professional wrestler on television, accustomed to the spotlight, wholly at ease in the combat zone. In the Homeric epic and its imitators, the hero's violent career finds its climax in an episode known as an *aristeia* (from Greek *aristos*, best; the same root gives us *aristocratic*). For a time, the hero takes centre stage on the battlefield in an adrenaline-charged killing spree. Burning brighter than all the rest, he blazes a path of magnificent destruction through the enemy ranks. It is terrifying to behold the warrior's bloody winning streak, his glorious dance of death, but it is also wondrous in its grace and virtuosity, like a prima ballerina's *pas seul* or a fiendishly difficult jazz solo.

Many of the world's epics are fascinated by the aesthetics of combat. The arming of the hero is a widespread motif, stretching back to the epics of the Canaanites and the Babylonians. Item by item, the bard paints a vivid portrait of the warrior in all his finery. Ready for battle, he stands splendidly arrayed, flushed with excitement. In the Homeric tradition, the hero's shield, forged by the gods, bears intricate engravings that the poet lovingly describes for dozens or hundreds of verses. Other epic heroes carry a signature weapon, sometimes with its own name and history, such as Arjuna's bow Gāṇḍīva, a divine reward for helping the god Agni destroy the Khandava forest, or Roland's sword Durendal, which was thought to contain a tooth of St Peter in its hilt. In full dress uniform, epic heroes are art objects, always in the public eye. Even those epics that depict war on a massive scale tend to imagine the fighting as a vast concatenation of heroic single combats. These, too, have their rituals, as the warriors introduce themselves, make demands, boast, threaten, taunt, and come to blows.

In African epic traditions, the villains are more likely to be supernatural agents, or to league with them, so that the hero must harness occult powers to defeat his enemies in battle. He gains mastery over his world not by sheer muscle but through his control of the hidden forces that animate the cosmos—a control which often takes the form of a magical tool or totem that enables him to defeat the villain's sorcery. In some versions of the West African *Sunjata* epic, for example, Sunjata takes back his homeland from the tyrant Soumaoro after learning how to exploit his enemy's only weakness, an arrow tipped with a cock's spur. There is a different kind of beauty in this display of power. But the key heroic ingredients are still there: will, violence, and pain. In the zero-sum logic of the martial epic, the only way to secure glory is to wrest it away from another by force.

Glory—*kleos* for the Greeks, from the verb *klyō*, to hear—underpins the warrior hero's code. His name is forged in the heat of conflict. The hero's status is public, quantifiable, and dependent on the evaluation of other men. He submits his violent deeds to the judgement of his community and appraises himself through their eyes. The war prizes that he earns, in turn, attract more followers to his retinue, further enhancing his stature. Yet warrior heroes are not just preening egotists who fight for personal vanity. We can better understand their pursuit of glory in its inverse form, as an intense fear of shame. To earn public dishonour could stain the warrior's family for generations. By fighting valorously, he repays a debt of honour to his ancestors and his community, and he passes on their legacy to his own children and grandchildren.

The war hero's high prestige, then, is a sort of provisional loan, and payments are always coming due. The Homeric warrior Sarpedon famously tells his kinsman Glaucus that they must fight on the front lines with their Trojan allies because those who would enjoy life's fleeting riches must earn them with deeds of honour. If he could live forever, he explains, he would not fight.

But since death comes to everyone, it is better that he should win glory in the time that remains. *Kleos* is a contract that the martial hero makes with death. He will throw himself into its jaws to attain the good name that is the only kind of immortality he knows. By the end of the *Iliad*, both Sarpedon and Glaucus will die fighting for Troy. And even those who most clearly see the limits of this heroic economy cannot find a way out of it: neither Achilles, who knows that only a fool would fight for a commander who has slighted him, nor Hector, who knows that Achilles' wrath will soon come for him, leaving his infant child without a father. These men are tragically unable to imagine some other model of selfhood, one that might not depend on this brutal exchange of pain for praise.

Civil war

Many epics around the world are stories of rage. With ornately crafted arms and armour, martial rituals, and heroic codes, warrior societies try to regulate this rage and make it beautiful. Nonetheless, the hero's anger risks spiralling out of control. Epic literature often dwells on what happens when the systems designed to manage heroic violence break down under pressure. War brings excesses of all kinds. Achilles ruthlessly defiles Hector's corpse, tying it to his chariot and dragging it around the tomb of his beloved Patroclus, whom Hector slew. The *olonkho* epics of the Yakuts describe the taking of head trophies from the battlefield. The *berserkir* of the Icelandic sagas, who may have a shadowy association with ancient Nordic bear cults, were said to storm into battle without armour, possessed by murderous fury and howling like wild animals. In the battle books that form the core of the *Mahābhārata*, the strongman Bhīma appals his friends and foes alike when he rips open the chest of his fallen enemy, Duḥśāsana, and drinks his blood.

Shockingly, Virgil's *Aeneid* portrays anger as a cosmic force that drives even the gods to destructive fury. Why, the poet asks, must his hero bear the goddess Juno's wrath? Why does she compel this man, so renowned for his piety, to endure so many hardships? Virgil never fully answers his own questions. The goddess's rage is implacable and beyond reason. Rising from some primitive abyss of divine evil, the *Aeneid*'s cosmic wrath finds expression in images of wind, storm, darkness, and, above all, fire. These symbols of nature at war with itself are a reminder that although Aeneas struggles to hold back the encroaching chaos, the gates of war cannot remain closed forever. Indeed, even Aeneas himself seems to succumb to *furor* in the poem's final moments, when he mercilessly thrusts his sword through the heart of his Rutulian rival, Turnus, as the defeated man kneels before him, lifting a hand in supplication.

Moreover, although war heroes safeguard their own people, they also threaten them. Anger is ungovernable. There is always a danger that the hero's overflowing torrent of rage will turn back against his own side. The *Iliad*, we recall, begins with strife, a deadly conflict that will drench the Troad with blood. Surprisingly, it is a quarrel not between Greeks and Trojans but between two commanders of the Greek army, Achilles and Agamemnon. When Agamemnon seizes for himself the captive woman Briseis, whom the Greeks had awarded to Achilles, he violates the deepest principle of their warrior society, which treats the spoils of war as symbolic extensions of a fighter's personal identity. Left to choose between killing Agamemnon or turning his back on the Greek war effort, Achilles withdraws. Many Greeks will die for Agamemnon's insult—and there can be no reconciliation because their honour economy is now broken beyond repair. Only revenge for his beloved friend Patroclus, slain by Hector, will make Achilles take up arms again. Over and over, in the world's epic literature, societies destroy themselves from within, torn apart by professional rivalries, family squabbles, and blood feuds.

The epic traditions of northern Europe also nourish deep root systems of civil conflict. In the Old English *Beowulf*, the hero rallies his human community against the monsters that would tear it apart. An uglier story comes into view, however, at the edges of this one. Glimpsed in the poem's ominous digressions, its fleeting memories of earlier times, its gloomy portents, its tales half-told in the firelight, this is a more familiar human story: a chronicle of old grudges, betrayals, raids, usurpations, revenge killings, broken families, and failed alliances. Grendel and his mother bring affliction to Heorot, the great mead hall of the Danish King Hrothgar—but angry men, not monsters, will one day burn it to ashes:

> The hall towered high,
> lofty and wide-gabled—fierce tongues of loathsome fire
> had not yet attacked it, nor was the time yet near
> when a mortal feud should flare between father-
> and son-in-law, sparked off by deeds of deadly enmity.

A breached oath, a family divided, a community on fire. The smell of kindred blood and burning thatch clung to medieval Germanic epics for many generations. In the final *aventiuren* of the *Nibelungenlied* (*c*.1200 CE), a poem that artfully blends an old heroic age revenge saga with Austro-Bavarian courtly romance, the ruthless Kriemhild schemes to burn alive the brothers-in-law who have murdered her husband Siegfried—their own act of revenge prompted long ago by an insult Kriemhild had hurled at their kinswoman Brünhild. When the two men escape her fiery trap, Kriemhild opts to behead them instead.

Further north, the red thread of the blood feud also weaves together many of the 13th-century Icelandic family sagas known as *Íslendinga sǫgur*. Set two or three centuries earlier, in the so-called Saga Age, these laconic prose tales typically open with a trifling provocation—an insult, an accident, a misunderstanding—that swells into violent conflict. Lives are lost; a cycle of revenge starts to unspool. The most fascinating aspect of these stories is their focus on how such cycles are broken. Peacekeeping and reconciliation count for more than heroic combat. Probably drawing on oral traditions that reach back to the early settlement of Iceland, the family sagas explore how those first homesteaders tamed their Wild West, building social and legal norms to keep the peace in a harsh landscape where men were well armed, quick-tempered, and loath to turn swords into ploughshares.

Everywhere, the world's epic canons tell stories of civil war. Family rivalry, factionalism, social fragmentation: these are the great themes of the *Mahābhārata*, the *Epic of Palnāḍu*, the *Tale of the Heike*, the *Sunjata*, the *Thebaid*, even the angelic rebellion in *Paradise Lost*. Perhaps the bitterest of them all is Lucan's *De Bello Civili* (*c.*61–5 CE). Composed in Virgil's shadow, this is an acidic anti-*Aeneid* that depicts Julius Caesar's war against the Roman Republic. Following the rebel general over the Rubicon, across southern Italy, and into Thessaly, where his army defeats the Republic's forces at the Battle of Pharsalus—hence the epic's popular nickname, the *Pharsalia*—the poet lashes out at his compatriots' monstrous perversion of martial glory:

> Of wars across Emathian plains, worse than civil wars,
> and of legality conferred on crime we sing, and of a mighty people
> attacking its own guts with victorious sword-hand,
> of kin facing kin, and, once the pact of tyranny was broken,
> of conflict waged with all the forces of the shaken world
> for universal guilt, and of standards raised in enmity against
> standards, of eagles matched and javelins threatening javelins.

No god or muse is summoned to tell this horror story. Its imagery is full of symmetrical pairings, kin facing kin, javelin against javelin, to show the insanity of a people going to war against themselves, as if punching their own reflection in a mirror. This is the poetry of an angry young man: gory, macabre, irreverent, a Quentin Tarantino epic for a world gone mad. Lucan has no heroes. His graphic imagery of human bodies torn and abused, starved, stabbed, beheaded, racked with disease, swollen to bursting, splattering the reader with blood, ghoulishly conveys the breakdown of the Roman body politic. Tragically, Lucan's own fate would force him, too, to turn violent hands against himself. Having joined a conspiracy to overthrow the emperor Nero, he was caught and compelled to take his own life at the age of 25, leaving unfinished this dark elegy for Roman liberty.

Holy war

For many readers, the Western epic tradition conjures up very different images of violence, scenes of glorious military conquest and empire building. It was the Romans who first conjoined epic and empire. Today, especially since the Vietnam War era, many scholars hear two voices in Virgil's *Aeneid*. One voice loudly proclaims Rome's destiny to rule the world; the other quietly mourns the lives lost or left behind by an empire in the making. For centuries, most of the poem's imitators heard the former voice alone. They noticed that the *Aeneid* weaves a tight pattern of binary oppositions to set its Trojan heroes apart from their many foes: order/chaos, unity/division, reason/passion, masculine/feminine, future/past. Scores of European war epics replicated Virgil's model, assailing their enemies with all the blind dogmatism and prejudice they could muster.

At the core of this epic ideology in Western Europe was the marriage of violence and religion. After the dissolution of the Western Roman Empire, new political and religious formations slowly coalesced in the Mediterranean world, spawning new identities and new literary forms. The spread of Christianity and Islam profoundly reshaped epic traditions across Europe, North Africa, the Near East, and Central Asia. By the 8th century CE, Islamic rule stretched from Spain to India, and a great Muslim trade network soon extended from the Atlantic Ocean to the South China Sea. The mounting pressure of Islamic expansionism, in turn, played a key role in forging a shared European consciousness. Thousands of small communities were drawn into a loose confederation under the Roman Catholic Church. In fact, the

Crusades of the 11th to 13th centuries had less impact on everyday life in the Middle East and the Levant than within Europe's own borders, where political and economic bonds were tightened, technologies of warfare refined, and religious minorities brutally persecuted in the name of a united Christendom on the march.

The new voice of Christian militarism rings bright and clear in the Old French *chansons de geste* (literally songs of deeds). These martial epics seem to have emerged shortly before or after the First Crusade of 1096–9, and they delighted Western Europe for several centuries. Roughly one hundred poems, largely anonymous, survive in manuscript. Most of them tell stories drawn from the age of Charlemagne; this body of legendary tales is often called the Matter of France, which medieval writers highly prized alongside the Matter of Britain (mostly concerning the knights of King Arthur) and the Matter of Rome (stories drawn from the Greco-Roman world). Perhaps rooted in the oral poetry of the popular minstrels known as *jongleurs*, the *chansons de geste* were composed or reworked by generations of clerics for an elite courtly audience with at least a nominal piety and a taste for adventure. Despite their backward-looking Carolingian setting, the new crusading spirit saturates many of these poems. Christianity's military triumphs over paganism and idolatry are a favourite theme. A few poems, like the *Chanson d'Antioche* and the *Chanson de Jérusalem*, narrate actual events from the Crusades. Others spin fabulous tales of heroic quests, colourful battles, and miraculous feats of derring-do as Charlemagne and his paladins clash with Saracens (and with one another) all over Europe in their efforts to mould a muscular Christian polity.

One of the earliest and greatest of these poems is the *Chanson de Roland*. In his 9th-century *Vita Karoli Magni*, the chronicler Einhard described a Basque attack on the rearguard of Charlemagne's army, commanded by his nephew and royal seneschal, Roland, as they crossed the Pyrenees en route from Spain in August 778. In the *Chanson de Roland*, the old story has changed: Roland is now a Frank, not a Breton. His Basque attackers have been transformed into Saracens. And this local border skirmish has become part of a great war of civilizations between Christians and Muslims across the Iberian Peninsula. Steeped in martial pageantry, the poem depicts its armed and caparisoned knights with remarkable technical detail and precision, but the sheer scale of its great battle swells to absurdity. A hundred thousand enemy soldiers wash over Roland's army, choking the mountain pass at Roncevaux with their dead.

It feels like an apocalyptic showdown between good and evil, and the feeling is reinforced by the poem's biblical allusions. God makes the sun stand still in the sky so that Charlemagne, like another Joshua, can avenge his fallen brethren. The Franks drive the Saracens before them to the Ebro River, where the pagans, crying useless prayers to their false gods, drown in their heavy armour—a parodic twist on the Israelites' miraculous deliverance at the Red Sea. Roland goes down fighting, but his martyrdom is a blood sacrifice acceptable to God, honouring his mandate to spread the church's worldly rule through holy war. The influence of stories like these was enormous. Translated into several languages, they bred endless adaptations and sequels. Their leading characters were portrayed on the stained-glass windows of European cathedrals. Adapted into pulpy romances, they were among the first literary fictions to issue from Gutenberg's printing press. For generations, epic knighthood in Western Europe rested on these twin pillars of rigid piety and belligerence, everywhere stained with infidel blood.

Technologies of war

The fiery partisanship of the *chansons de geste* grossly distorts the true relations between medieval Europe and the Muslim world. The real story was shaped by violent confrontation but also by diplomacy, trade, and artistic exchange—forces on display, for example, in the sacred epic of Ethiopia, *Kebra Nagast* (*c.*14th century CE), which weaves together Jewish, Christian, and Islamic cultural traditions as it traces Ethiopia's ruling dynasty back to the union of King Solomon and the Queen of Sheba. Even the code of chivalry itself, which flourished for centuries in the heroic literature of Western Europe, was partly based on the ideals of equestrian knighthood (*furūsiyya*) cultivated by Muslim Arabs in the Near East and North Africa. In the 12th and 13th centuries, as European dreams of reconquering the Holy Land receded into memory, the Carolingian heroic legends evolved into new forms. Tight-lipped war epics gave way to the sprawling, interlaced plotlines of courtly romances. Arthurian folklore from the British Isles seeped into the Matter of France, and erotic desire found its way into the epic hero's consciousness. The warrior's creed began to police the hero's conduct both on and off the battlefield, promoting new codes of courtesy, liberality, and elegant self-display in courtly spheres that lent growing authority to women. With their iridescent dreams of love and enchantment, tales of chivalry that blended the Carolingian and Arthurian traditions spread all over Europe. Among their many forms were the popular Franco-Italian folk poems known as *cantari cavallereschi*; these later found a home in the humanist courtly circles of Renaissance Italy, where poets such as Matteo Maria Boiardo, Ludovico Ariosto, and Torquato Tasso fused them together with the Greco-Roman epic tradition to create the magnificent romance epics of the 16th century.

It is an odd quirk of history that the rise of those great chivalric epics coincided with the decline of the European warrior aristocracy who cut such a graceful figure in their pages. We might compare these poems to the Westerns of early American cinema, whose wandering gunslingers—the distant offspring of these old knights errant—were already receding into myth. The reasons for the fall of the fighting knighthood in late medieval Europe are many, from the growing power of centralized monarchies to the outflow of wealth from baronial estates into urban capital markets. But no less crucial was a revolution in military technology. The knowledge of gunpowder had reached Europe from Asia by the early 14th century. During the Hundred Years War (1337–1453), formerly impregnable city walls shattered under the onslaught of heavy artillery barrages, which could fire cannonballs weighing as much as five tons. Guns changed everything. The military supremacy of the knight on horseback had relied on technical improvements in armour and weaponry in the early Middle Ages, when heavy cavalry units began to appear on European battlefields. The culture of chivalric knighthood depended on the warhorse (both *chivalry* and *cavalry* derive from the late Latin word *caballus*, horse), and on the tactical advantages that mounted warriors enjoyed over lightly armed foot soldiers. As gunpowder weapons grew more potent and acquired greater range, those advantages crumbled. Even Lancelot would have been no match for a disciplined infantry formation armed with muskets.

Epic traditions are conservative, designed to resist change. Wary of new technologies, epics tend to absorb them slowly, selectively, without discarding the old. In Homer's *Iliad*, for example, most of the Greek warriors seem to carry small, round shields, resembling the hoplite shields that came into use around 700 BCE. Yet the hero Ajax still carries a massive tower shield, which had been used in Mycenaean warfare at least 700 years before. In similar fashion, firearms have gradually crept into the folk epics of Central Asia, such as the Kyrgyz *Manas* and the Nart sagas of the northern Caucasus. The gun has also been slowly reshaping African oral epic traditions. In the Bamana *Epic of Almami Samori Touré*, a story about the Islamic empire builder who fought French colonial rule in West Africa, the genies give Touré the first firearms to fall into African hands. And in certain retellings of the *Sunjata* epic, the totemic cock's spur that defeats the sorcerer Soumaoro is not fashioned into an arrow but fired from a gun.

In Western Europe, the gunpowder revolution posed an acute problem for epic poets. The Greco-Roman heroes strove for glory in single combat, testing arm against brawny arm. Where was the glory in anonymous mass warfare? Many poets, choosing to look away from the carnage, sealed off their poems against the modern world. Guns are absent from most of the great chivalric epics, such as Torquato Tasso's *Gerusalemme Liberata* (1581) and Edmund Spenser's *Faerie Queene* (1596). But some epic poets did embrace them. Shipborne cannons played a part in epics about maritime combat, for example, such as those portraying the Battle of Lepanto. In colonial epics, too, we find gun-toting Europeans leading ground campaigns in Africa or the Americas, where cavalry units played a minor role. On those faraway shores, artillery warfare by land and sea could prop up fantasies of technological supremacy over indigenous peoples from the Indian Ocean to the New World.

Guns on European soil were another matter. Poets well knew the threat they posed to heroic literature. Ludovico Ariosto's sparkling romance epic *Orlando Furioso* has little patience for old chivalric pieties. Ariosto reimagines the famous Roland as a rampaging madman, driven insane by his love for a beautiful pagan princess. He regains his sanity only when a trusty friend journeys to the moon to retrieve the hero's lost wits. But the poem turns serious when Ariosto lashes out against gunpowder weapons. Guns, he complains, enable the low-born to defeat their social betters; they render useless the knight's courage, skill, and grace; they are tools of cowardice and fraud. As Ariosto recognized, this was not just a new kind of firepower. It marked the rise of a new social order. Anonymous violence on an industrial scale was eating away at the feudal past. The elite warrior caste that had ruled Western Europe for centuries was fading into fiction, locked away forever in the enchanted castle of Ariosto's poem.

Ariosto blamed the devil himself for putting the technology of gunpowder into human hands. This was a widespread belief in Renaissance Europe. Its fullest expression came in John Milton's

Paradise Lost, where Satan invents heavy artillery during his war against the loyal angels in heaven. His demonic cannon fire is grotesque and scatological:

> those deep-throated engines belched, whose roar
> Embowelled with outrageous noise the air,
> And all her entrails tore, disgorging foul
> Their devilish glut, chained thunderbolts and hail
> Of iron globes, which on the victor host
> Levelled, with such impetuous fury smote,
> That whom they hit, none on their feet might stand,
> Though standing else as rocks, but down they fell
> By thousands, angel on archangel rolled.

With his nauseating imagery of digestion and bodily discharge, Milton captures the unnatural horror of the rebel angels' war machine, which mangles and weaponizes God's creation. A ghoulish anachronism is on display here, a mismatch between the devils' old-fashioned thirst for epic glory and their new, high-tech weapons of mass destruction. Unlike Ariosto, Milton had no interest in propping up a dying aristocratic ideology. He was criticizing the very idea of heroic violence. His war in heaven made a lasting impact on Europe's mock epic tradition, which gleefully exposed the breakdown of the old epic contract—blood for glory, pain for praise—in an era of wrenching technological change.

The battle's aftermath

Martial epics are not just triumphal pageants and ticker-tape parades. They tell stories of affliction and loss. Many of the world's great war epics end with tears. Time is granted for the survivors to remember the fallen and consign their bodies to death. Bereaved widows lament their uncertain future. Sometimes there are ceremonial sacrifices or funeral games. Expiatory rites might be needed to mollify the angry dead. The *Chanson de Roland*, for all its partisan bigotry, lingers over the grief of both Christians and Muslims as they tally their appalling losses at Roncevaux. Although the Russian *Tale of Igor's Campaign* (*c*.1187) ends with the ransom and liberation of its war hero, Prince Igor, the story's melancholy climax belongs to his wife Iaroslavna, who stands at dawn on the ramparts of Putivl and mourns her reckless husband's defeat in battle:

> O wind, why do you, my lord wind,
> blow so fiercely?
> Why do you bring on your light wings
> Kuman arrows against the warriors of my beloved?
> Is it not enough for you to blow under the clouds,
> to loll the ships on the blue sea?
> Why, my lord, did you scatter my joy
> over the feathergrass of the prairie?

Likewise, a vast swath of the *Mahābhārata* concerns the gloomy aftermath of its 18-day Kurukshetra war. The Pāṇḍavas have defeated their unjust cousins, the Kauravas, but they have drenched India with blood and lost nearly everyone they love. Even a sacred horse sacrifice that should atone for their wrongs does little to assuage the guilt gnawing at Yudhishthira, son of Dharma, who has no desire to rule the kingdom he has won at such an intolerable cost. Epics preserve the story of a people, a story shaped by suffering as well as by triumph. They remind us that some dreams are beyond our reach and some losses cannot be restored.

Near the end of the *Iliad*, night has fallen over Troy. The blaze of Patroclus' funeral pyre has gone dark and his bones have been laid in the earth. Yet the wrath of Achilles still smoulders. He has denied himself food and sleep. Inconsolable, he seems more in love with death than life. For twelve days he has abused Hector's corpse, a sick ritual of vengeance that has failed to ease his misery. Now, aided by the gods, the Trojan King Priam gathers a

3. Priam's ransom of Hector, from a terracotta hydria (water jar) of the early 6th century BCE.

costly ransom. He secretly travels deep behind enemy lines. Slipping into Achilles' tent, he grasps the knees of his foe. He implores Achilles to give back Hector's body so that the grieving king may at last bury his son (see Figure 3). The Greek warrior ponders the old man who crouches at his feet, kissing the hands that killed his child. Achilles also, Priam reminds him, has a father who loves him—a father who, Achilles knows, will never see him again, for his own cruel fate is to die young and far from home. Tears well in his eyes, and both men start to weep:

> Taking hold of the old man's hand he gently pushed him away;
> they both remembered their own, Priam crouched at Achilles'
> feet and weeping without ceasing for man-slaying Hector,
> while Achilles wept for his own father, and then again for
> Patroclus; and their groaning went up, spreading through the hut.

It is a fleeting moment of communion for two souls joined in pain. The Trojan king starts to draw Achilles back toward life and human fellowship. The hero's feverish obsession with Hector's corpse finally breaks. He accepts the ransom and yields up the body. Now he urges Priam to eat and sleep, for mourning must not last forever. Soon enough, Greek and Trojan warriors will take up arms again. But the *Iliad*, like so much of the world's epic literature, never forgets the cost of war. The heroism and the heartache are both part of its story.

Chapter 5
Family ties

Virgil's *Aeneid* (19 BCE) tells the story of Aeneas, the legendary founder of Rome. He is a Trojan refugee, forced to flee his homeland when the Greeks lay waste to Troy. Aeneas sets sail for Italy with a huddled mass of traumatized migrants. They cling to an unlikely prophecy: Jupiter has decreed that the children of this weary vagabond will one day rule the world. As Aeneas wanders the Mediterranean Sea, a lonely hero begrimed with blood and sea salt, he must bear the burden of his people's destiny. Stranded between Troy and Rome, he will sacrifice everything he once knew, and nearly everyone he loves, to lay the foundations of an empire he will not live to see.

Early in the epic, when Aeneas recalls his last desperate hours in Troy, he summons one of the poem's most unforgettable images. The city is on fire. Screams tear the air as Greeks butcher Trojans in the streets. Resolving to flee Troy, Aeneas takes the hand of his son, Iulus, and calls on his elderly father, Anchises, to join them. But Anchises stubbornly refuses to leave his devastated homeland. So Aeneas hoists up the old man and carries him on his shoulders. It is a famous tableau: the pious family man, flanked by father, son, and spouse. On his back Aeneas literally bears his precious Trojan ancestry, which will live on in his own child—and, some day, in his Roman progeny. The best of his children's children shall be the emperor Augustus Caesar, portrayed by Virgil as Aeneas' direct lineal descendant. The genealogy makes little historical sense, but that hardly matters. Virgil gives his people a simple and potent origin myth, forming world history into a providential design that stretches from the Trojan War to the Pax Romana. The outlines of that design can already be seen in the family portrait described above, which was to endure for centuries in European visual art (see Figure 4).

4. **Aeneas flees Troy with his family, from an enamel plaque by the anonymous Master of the *Aeneid*, c.1530–5, based on woodcut illustrations by the printer Johann Grüninger.**

Traditional epic heroes tend to be loners. They are exiles and iconoclasts, solitary chieftains, unruly vassals, monster-slaying nomads, guns for hire. Eyes fixed on the far horizon, they show little interest in domestic attachments. And yet the world's epics are obsessed with family, clan, and ancestry. They chart the lineages of tribes or nations. Some heap praise on the real or imaginary forebears of a ruler or patron. Others unearth the causes of old family feuds. Many epics portray sibling rivalries or conflicts between the old and the young. They might also linger over a father's hopes for his newborn child, or the anguish of a mother whose son lies cold on a battlefield far from home.

It is no wonder that epic storytellers care so deeply about kinship. The family tethers the hero to a community—and sometimes brings the two into conflict. Epics often probe the social obligations that knit families together or tear them apart. In many cases, the family also draws the epic hero into contact with human sexuality and gender relations. At first glance, many of the world's epics might look like barren islands of masculinity, far from the fertile shores of the domestic novel. But no story that would chronicle the whole life of a society can silence women's voices. Nor can it omit the vital business of love, sex, and procreation that looms so large in the human experience, although it might push those concerns to the margins of the hero's biography.

Fathers and sons

As stories of kinship, epics preserve the names and pedigrees of important ancestors. The plainest way to record those lineages is to sort them into a list. A famous instance is Homer's catalogue of ships in the *Iliad*, a sprawling census of 1,186 Achaean vessels and the warriors they bore to Troy. Many other epics break off their heroic action from time to time so they can unspool their characters' family lines from prehistory to the present day. Virgil's Aeneas, for example, visits the underworld in search of his father Anchises, who grants him a prophetic vision of his Roman descendants. The episode was doggedly imitated by the dynastic epics of the Renaissance era, poems written to celebrate the rise of an aristocratic clan or royal house. The poets aim to flatter their patrons with these rollcalls of illustrious names. They are also a form of public record-keeping, like a genealogical register or a calendar of state papers. We might expect authors toiling in royal libraries or courtly archives to compile these ceremonial lists. But traditional oral epics, too, such as the *Epic of Mali Bero*, the story of the Zarma people of Niger, can devote thousands of verses to tracing the patrimony of their ruling elites.

Epic traditions set individual heroic achievement inside the larger story of a clan or bloodline over time. However, epic singers are selective in how they narrate the past. They compress the histories of nations into the deeds of a few powerful magnates. Great intertribal conflicts are traced back to quarrels between rival brothers, or husbands and wives, or parents and children. Epics of civil war sometimes find their origins in a ruling family divided against itself. Popular throughout the Middle Ages, for example, was Statius' *Thebaid* (*c.*80–92 CE), a bleak Silver Age Roman epic in which the city of Thebes is ravaged by a power struggle between the two cursed sons of Oedipus, Eteocles and Polyneices—the death throes of a family with no future.

Epic storytellers take a special interest in the relationship between father and son. Of all family bonds, this one carries the greatest political consequences, at least in societies that are patriarchal (bestowing social authority on male heads of household) and patrilinear (channelling the flow of power from those men to their male offspring). Father–son relationships form crucial pressure points in this system. On them depends the orderly handover of wealth and title across generations. Any such transfer of power is a highly sensitive event in the life of a community. Also at stake are profound questions about human identity. Is a child's fate governed by the parents' choices? Does a son become fully himself by carrying on his father's legacy or by breaking away from the father?

In traditional epics all over the world, we find hostile fathers who torment their children. In one popular scenario, a ruler tries to destroy his own son, often in response to a prophecy that the child will some day overthrow or kill him. Some epics use other male figures—a scheming uncle, perhaps—as symbolic stand-ins for these murderous fathers. Anthropologists tell us that father–son conflicts are common in stratified warrior societies, where the young are driven to wrest power from their elders by force. Deeper human instincts might also be in play. It is hard for a big man to see his own greatness outshone by a hero child. Maybe these vaguely Oedipal tales give voice to the unspoken resentment that fathers feel when they find themselves displaced by the next generation, if only because it reminds them of their own mortality. Every son, from this point of view, is a kind of parricide.

In the son's eyes, meanwhile, the murderous father could symbolize the inhospitable universe into which humanity is born, one that the child must somehow outwit, bargain, or coerce into a home. Such a son is Mwindo, a legendary hero of the Nyanga people who dwell in the eastern rainforests of the Democratic Republic of the Congo. This rich storytelling region forms part of a vast sub-Saharan cultural area that has been called the African epic belt, stretching for thousands of miles from the Atlantic coast of Senegambia to the African Great Lakes. Several versions of the Mwindo epic cycle, performed by Nyanga bards known as *kárisi*, were transcribed by Western scholars in the 1950s and 1960s. The variant that shines the brightest light on fathers and sons begins in the mythical village of Tubondo, nestled in a remote forest region called Ihímbí. The local chief, Shemwindo, demands that none of his wives shall bear a son. All obligingly give birth to daughters, except for his favourite wife, whose long, strange pregnancy brings Mwindo into the world.

When Shemwindo learns of the secret birth, he tries to murder the boy in ever more outlandish ways: he throws a spear into his hut; buries him alive; cages him inside a drum and hurls it into a river. Unfazed and indestructible, singing cheerfully inside his drum, Mwindo embarks on a dangerous underwater journey to seek out his paternal aunt, who is married to the water serpent Mukiti. Wielding his magical conga sceptre and aided by his supernatural relatives, Mwindo marches on Tubondo and burns it to the ground. He chases his fleeing father to the underworld, where Mwindo defeats a menagerie of gods and monsters to lay hands on him. Back in Tubondo, Mwindo resurrects the slain villagers, Shemwindo makes a public apology, and the two hammer out a power-sharing arrangement to rule as father and son. More adventures follow, but Mwindo's core trials of identity have been overcome. To be sure, this wronged son is no hand-wringing Hamlet. He springs from his mother's womb full of laughter and aggression. Bellowing his independence to the universe, the child gives himself the name *Kábútwa-kénda* (the Little-one-just-born-he-walked). Still, for all his bravado, the whole trajectory of his heroic life aims toward a reckoning with his hostile father, and the journey enmeshes him in a web of kin relations that affirm Mwindo's bonds with family, community, and cosmos.

The epic's fascination with filicide can take subtler forms. One variation on this theme, found across the Indo-European world, is a haunting tale of misrecognition. Fate draws a father and son into a deadly single combat, and neither man knows the other's identity until it is too late. Nowhere is the story told with such melancholy grandeur as in Abolqasem Ferdowsi's *Shahnameh*. Searching for his lost horse, the warrior-hero Rostam visits Samangan in the region of Turan. The king's daughter Tahmina falls in love with him and visits him by night, hoping to bear his child. She conceives; Rostam returns home, never to see her again. He leaves her a bracelet to give to their unborn child as a token of their union. Tahmina bears a son and names him Sohrab. In due time, she reveals to her son, who has by now become a powerful fighter, that the mighty Rostam is his father. When Turan goes to war against Iran, Sohrab longs to meet Rostam and to unite the two kingdoms under their rule. Through a series of tragic missteps, both men fail to identify each other on the battlefield. They face off in single combat as the two armies' fiercest champions. For days, the heavy blows fall. Both men exhaust themselves. Sohrab, strangely drawn toward his enemy, feels growing unease. But Rostam is implacable; he fatally stabs the youth. The dying Sohrab gasps that his father Rostam will some day avenge his death. He reaches for his mother's bracelet and the awful recognition comes.

There is a similar tale in the Armenian folk epic *David of Sassoun*, where the father utters an awful curse against his son Mher before seeing the golden ring that proves his identity. Even further from the Iranian frontier, other variants include the Irish Ulster Cycle (Cú Chulainn slays his son Connla), the Indian *Mahābhārata* (a son, Babruvahana, kills his father Arjuna), and the Old High German *Hildebrandslied*. This fragmentary heroic poem survives in a single manuscript, copied at the Benedictine monastery of Fulda in the early 9th century CE. The poem's 68 surviving verses find the two men preparing for battle. This time, the son, Hadubrand, readily declares his name and parentage. But he refuses to believe that the enemy standing before him is his father, since he has heard that Hildebrand is dead. The old warrior sees the young man's burning defiance. In his heart, Hildebrand seems to weigh the cost to his prestige of backing down from the fight. Fate, he concludes, has brought them to this moment; may the best man win. Father and son come to blows as the fragment breaks off. With gloomy fatalism, the poem brings two forces into hopeless opposition: the unbending laws of a martial honour culture pitted against a parent's love for his child. There can be no victor. Perhaps these terrible acts of violence only repeat, in a different form, the cruelty of abandoning an unborn son to grow up without a father. Epic heroes might neglect their family ties, but they cannot wholly sever the bonds of kinship that join other human lives to their own.

Of course, we also witness deep parental love in the world's epics, and moments of tender domesticity, as when the *Iliad*'s Hector and Andromache laugh to see their infant son shrink in fear from his father's plumed war helmet. And the hero is nearly always entangled in a thick skein of family relations, not just those of parent and child. Times of crisis can either fray or tighten those attachments. Loners or not, epic heroes may be spouses, grandparents, second cousins. Their kin have a stake in their mission and contribute to its outcome. In the *Ozidi Saga*, an epic of the Ijo people of Nigeria performed by Okabou Ojobolo in the early 1960s, the hero Ozidi battles fourteen foes, one by one, to avenge the murder of his father and rise to supreme power in his homeland. But it is Ozidi's grandmother, the sorceress Oreame, who magically blunts his enemies' attacks, finds the taboo items he needs to defeat them, re-attaches his head when it is lopped off, and, when all is over, accepts his sword as a pledge that he is done with violence. At the story's climax, when Ozidi combats the mighty Smallpox King, only the healing ministrations of his mother and grandmother can save his life and secure his victory—a lingering memory, perhaps, of the traditionally matrilineal culture of the Ijo. In epic traditions elsewhere, a wife or nephew or companion at arms might share the spotlight in this way. Many hands shape the hero's destiny, and the epic is their story too.

Dido's daughters

When Virgil's Aeneas hurries his family from the burning ruins of Troy, his wife Creusa trails behind the menfolk. Aeneas looks back—but she is gone. Distraught, the hero runs back into the flames to find her. He is too late. Creusa was not meant to leave her Trojan birthplace. Her ghostly form rises before Aeneas in the darkness. She charges him to bring their child to a new home far away, where a new queen awaits the hero. Three times Aeneas tries to embrace his wife, but the phantom slips through his fingers. Creusa is not the last woman Aeneas will leave behind on his journey to the destined shores of Latium. His fate will kick away the supports that once sustained him—home, parents, wife, lover, crewmates, friends, and allies—as he walks a lonely path toward empire. Aeneas' struggle to master his world is also a quest to conquer himself. He will learn to brace himself against loss and grief with a taut self-discipline that answers only to the gods' will. As Creusa has foretold, another marriage will come one day. But it will be a chilly, political affair. Aeneas' future bride, the Latin princess Lavinia, does not speak a word in Virgil's epic.

Epic heroes rarely have a sex life. Most seem far more concerned with man-to-man comradeship or rivalry. Many traditional epics do portray the male hero's efforts to acquire a bride, sometimes through diplomacy, often by force. Nonetheless, erotic desire does not much afflict these men. It is as if their social lives had stalled at some early stage of sexual maturation, like pre-adolescent boys who would rather play *Call of Duty* than go to the school dance. In the Western epic tradition, alluring women often stand in the male hero's path and make him stumble on his way. Their real menace, however, lies not so much in their sexuality as in the threats they pose to patriarchal authority. It is no coincidence that many are supernatural beings who outmatch the physical strength of mortal men. In the *Epic of Gilgamesh*, the hero spurns the sexual advances of the goddess Ishtar, who embodies both erotic love and war, and then faces her wrath. The refusals multiply in Homer's *Odyssey*, as Odysseus wrests himself from the snares of one otherworldly female after another—Calypso, Circe, the Sirens—to take back his rightful place as husband of Penelope and lord of Ithaca. Some scholars believe that even the beautiful Helen of Troy, whose broken marriage incites the events of Homer's *Iliad*, was worshipped as a vegetation goddess in Mycenaean Greece. Under the influence of Greek lyric poetry and tragic drama, epic poets learned to probe more deeply into the minds and hearts of these powerful women. An influential early model is Apollonius' *Argonautica*: while Jason is an oddly bland hero, the Colchean princess Medea is an enthralling chiaroscuro portrait of a young woman in love with the Greek stranger. But it is

The Epic

a portrait tinged with traces of witchcraft, necromancy, and barbarism, hinting at a doomed marriage and a shocking revenge left untold by Apollonius' unfinished poem.

The tragic women of Apollonius and Euripides loom behind Virgil's Dido, Queen of Carthage. Her restless ghost has long haunted Western literary history. Doomed by the gods to fall in love with her tempest-tossed Trojan guest, she endures all the ecstasies and torments of desire, abandonment, despair, and death, slain by her own hand as another sacrifice to Aeneas' divine mission. Scores of artists and thinkers have brooded over Dido's tragic suicide. St Augustine wept for her. Chaucer and Shakespeare eulogized her. A mountain in Antarctica is named after her. But if she is a martyr to Aeneas' Roman destiny, she also threatens it. As a charismatic queen, Dido disrupts a cosmic order that aligns itself with the ambitions of empire-building men. We often see Virgil's Dido at night, swathed in darkness, linked with dreams and the irrational. Virgil hints that, like Medea, she might traffic in black magic. Her unnatural death seems to unleash a nameless demonic energy into the universe. With her last breath, Dido assails her faithless lover with a curse: an eternal hatred shall kindle into war between Carthage and Rome. This painful reminder of the Punic Wars would also have put Virgil's audience in mind of another menacing African queen, Cleopatra, who had enfeebled Roman manhood and plunged the Mediterranean world into war.

The women of the *Aeneid* characteristically look backward. They are mourners of the dead. They stand for memory, for what has been lost or forsaken. Aeneas will encounter both Creusa and Dido in the underworld, forever cut off from the flow of time, before he makes his way to Latium. Dido's curse shows that memory is also the engine of revenge. With its psychology of futile repetition, Dido's vengeance draws her into an alliance with the goddess Juno—Jupiter's headstrong wife, bent on thwarting his divine plan for Aeneas—and the chthonic female forces that serve her primitive rage. Fixated on the past, Virgil's women are also self-destructive. Dido thrusts a Trojan sword into her own breast, compulsively re-enacting her betrayal by Aeneas as a lover and political ally. As her city erupts in flames, Dido transforms Carthage into another burning Troy that the hero must leave behind.

The Virgilian epic tradition is filled with Dido's daughters. Abandoned women walk through Western epic history in endless postures of loss and mourning. Early Christian readers of the *Aeneid* strongly associated them with sexual passion and its power to enthrall the minds of men. In early modern Europe, when the literary romances of Celtic Britain merged with the Virgilian epic canon, they transformed these women into supernatural *femmes fatales*. Poets such as Boiardo, Ariosto, Tasso, and Spenser crafted a hybrid species of chivalric romance epic that forced its heroes to choose between love and war. A new kind of sexy sorceress, tracing her lineage partly to Dido and Medea, partly to Homer's Circe, and partly to Morgan le Fay, lured unsuspecting knights into amorous pleasure gardens, island paradises, or bowers of bliss. Rooted in the ancient literary tradition of the *locus amoenus* (pleasant place), these are erotic cocoons of ease and rest, womblike retreats where the hero can lay down the heavy burden of making history. In Torquato Tasso's *Gerusalemme Liberata* (1581), a bathing nymph entices the Christian crusaders to disarm and frolic with her:

> This is the world's safe harbor, a place of rest
> from all its cares, and here you may enjoy
> the pleasures known to free and untamed men
> once, long ago, in the golden age.
> Those weapons of war you needed in times past
> can now be safely laid aside
> and consecrated to the silence of these shades,
> for here you shall be warriors of love alone.

It is a dreamy, lawless paradise, a false Eden that calls the hero back to nature, to childhood, to the libidinal depths of his own unconscious. The seductive women who govern these places tempt the hero with sexual and political freedom. But what they really offer, the poets insist, is enthrallment to female authority, a prison of infantile dependency. In the masculinist logic of the chivalric epic, heroic men must break free from these enclaves of repose, shun the magical ladies who made them, and plunge back with new resolve into the flow of history.

Warrior maidens, heroic wives

Although women rarely play starring roles in epic narratives, they frequently help or hinder the causes of men. Many, like Virgil's Dido, are figures of great imaginative force, straining against their secondary roles as the hero's allies or antagonists. Still, the world's epics typically uphold traditional institutions and power structures. When transgressive women burst through the social codes that constrict their freedom, uncomfortable feelings are unleashed, and punishment soon follows. 'Was she thy God,' the Son asks Adam in *Paradise Lost*, after Eve has fed him the forbidden fruit, 'that to her | Thou didst resign thy manhood?' It is often the hero's task to crack down on women who jeopardize male prerogatives. Few stories better capture these women's scandalous allure—and their violent suppression—than the tale of Poi-Soya-un-mat, an oral epic of the Ainu people of Hokkaido, Japan. The hero, Otasam-Un-Kur, learns that he is betrothed to the infamous woman of Poi-Soya, a troublemaking tomboy who dresses like a man, neglects her needlework, and bullies the menfolk of her village. Otasam-Un-Kur's heroism largely consists of beating his wife senseless after each new act of defiance. It is clear that her behavior violates deeply held social taboos. The poem's title, *Poi-Soya-un-mat shipitonere shikamuinere*, can be translated as 'The Woman of Poi-Soya Makes Herself a God.' But the gender dynamics of this Wife of Bath's tale are hard to assess. In the story's five overlapping sections, the characters take turns narrating the action from their own points of view. One of those speakers is the woman of Poi-Soya herself. She graphically describes her husband's abuse:

> I was beaten violently,
> and my heart grew faint
> with the mortal agony of it.
> After that,
> I felt him slashing me,
> I felt him tearing me,
> and my heart was faint
> with the mortal agony of it.
> After that,
> he continued to beat me,
> and I felt him striking me,
> I felt him slashing me,
> and excruciating pains
> gripped my insides.

This vivid first-person testimony calls to mind the Ainu tradition of women's epics (*menoko yukar*), a cycle of stories usually voiced by female relatives of the heroic epics' male characters. The poem's gender politics are still more uncertain because its first published edition was transcribed from a performance by a female reciter, Hiraga Etenoa, from the village of Shin-Piraka in October 1932. Etenoa was among the most gifted epic singers in the region, where a strict gendered division of labour allowed women to flourish as bards and shamans while men devoted their time to hunting and fishing. To hear a female poet reciting these verses might draw a mixed-gender audience into unexpected vectors of empathy and identification.

Nonetheless, the epic hero's encounters with strong women usually end in violence. A scorned lover kills herself; a king puts his scheming queen to the sword; a witch cowers in fear while a knight hacks apart her enchanted garden. Sometimes men and women

82

even take up arms and bring these power struggles to the battlefield. A special intrigue swirls around the female warrior. Fighting a literal battle of the sexes, she spills men's blood and breaks their traditional monopoly on physical force. We find her in many cultural traditions, from the Amazons of Greco-Roman mythology to the shield-maidens of Old Norse sagas and the *polenitsas* of the Russian *byliny*. Some of these warrior women might have sprung from ancient contacts with matriarchal cultures. Others might have been inspired by real-life fighting women such as Boudicca, the Celtic queen who led a revolt against the Romans, or Hangaku Gozen, the Japanese *onna-musha* warrior, or dozens of others who have left their mark on world history. Or they might simply recall those harrowing moments in wartime when wives have armed themselves alongside their husbands and sons in a last desperate defence of their homeland.

Wherever they arise, the epic's fighting women stoke complex fantasies of male disempowerment. It should not surprise us that these women are typically virgins who scorn romantic entanglements with men. Love is war, the poets say. Age-old metaphors for unrequited desire—the lover slain by a lady's heart-wounding eyes—are made painfully real when these women's sharp spears pierce men's flesh. In their chaste militancy, prickly, unattainable, they both fascinate and menace. Some scholars have wondered whether they embody men's anxieties about the rising economic status or political agency of women. It is clear, at least, that the epic holds these women at a distance from everyday social relations. They tend to have exotic origin stories that cordon them off from other women. Many have absent mothers. In Virgil's *Aeneid*, the Volscian warrior queen Camilla grew up in the wilderness with her exiled father. Devoted to the virginal goddess Diana, she was nursed as an infant by a wild mare. Virgil's followers picked up the theme. The Saracen lady knight Marfisa, in Ariosto's *Orlando Furioso*, was suckled by a lioness; Clorinda, an Ethiopian warrior in Tasso's *Gerusalemme Liberata*, by a tigress. Yet even though they are marked as outliers, untouched by civilized norms, these women pose radical questions about gender identity. In patriarchal cultures that deem it natural law to give men the sword and women the sewing needle, the female warrior should be an impossibility. Her easy dominance in the most masculine of all arenas, the theatre of war, dares audiences to ask whether their gender categories derive from nature or culture, necessity or desire.

The woman warrior might be less subversive than she seems, however, since her wild freedom usually comes to an abrupt end in death or marriage. In the Western epic tradition, she tends to team up with the hero's enemies, who are associated with social disorder, pluralism, and womanhood. Quintus of Smyrna's *Posthomerica* (*c.*4th century CE), drawing on lost tales from the Greek epic cycle, tells how Achilles slew the Amazon warrior queen Penthesilea, only to fall in love with his victim when he took off her helmet and saw her beauty in death—that is, when he no longer posed an active threat to men. In another widely copied scene, Virgil's Camilla cuts a swathe through the Trojan army in the *Aeneid*'s climactic battle. She sets her sights on a Phrygian warrior gorgeously adorned with Eastern purple and gold. Any male soldier would have coveted such war trophies, but it is a woman's craving for finery, according to Virgil, that inflames Camilla. Distracted, she fails to notice a Trojan ally stalking her from afar. His spear fatally impales her virgin breast.

Other traditions show strongwomen being disciplined through marriage. Adopting a common folktale motif, the *Nibelungenlied*'s Brünhild challenges her suitors to trials of strength. When the Burgundian king Gunther wins those athletic contests with secret aid from the mighty Siegfried, Brünhild is suspicious. Refusing to consummate their marriage, she ties up Gunther and hangs him from the wall of their wedding chamber. Once again, though, Siegfried brings Brünhild under the patriarchal yoke, this time by donning his invisibility cloak and forcibly restraining her while Gunther (or possibly Siegfried himself) lays claim to the new bride.

Nor do all warrior women shun a husband's embraces. The lady knights Bradamante and Britomart, in Ariosto's *Orlando Furioso* and Spenser's *Faerie Queene*, strap on their armour and ride into the wilderness not to battle the patriarchy but to hunt down their destined bridegrooms. They will become the legendary foremothers of the poets' dynastic patrons.

Marriage itself can be a heroic enterprise. At the heart of Homer's *Odyssey* are a husband and wife struggling to reforge their union after many years apart. Odysseus is a trickster, kept alive by wit and wiles in an alien world. But so is Penelope, left behind in Ithaca and plagued by importunate suitors. Her famous stratagem to keep these men at bay—promising to remarry after she has finished weaving her father-in-law's funeral shroud, but secretly unweaving each day's work by night—is also a private dream of undoing the passage of time, denying the growth to manhood of their son Telemachus, wishing the Trojan War unfought. In a sense, time does stand still at Ithaca. Penelope's gloomy stasis is much like Odysseus' inert longing on the island of Calypso, where he spends his days weeping by the seashore for his lost wife and home. They are two of a kind. The poem is crowded with wicked wives, Helen, Clytemnestra, Aphrodite, whose infidelity to their husbands makes them a rogues' gallery of anti-Penelopes, highlighting the heroic pain and effort of her own constancy.

When an unknown beggar arrives at her door, Penelope feels it is time to arrange a folkloric bride contest. The man who can string Odysseus' bow and drive an arrow through twelve axes shall marry her. By passing the test with ease, the disguised Odysseus woos and wins his wife for a second time, proving his dominance over the men of Ithaca. But Penelope shares her husband's *mētis* (Homer's term for cunning ingenuity), and she has a more intimate test for him. Alone with him at last, she asks her maid to prepare his old bed outside their bedroom. Odysseus cries out in anger. Who has moved their bed? The thing is impossible. He carved the bed with his own hands from a living olive tree, built their bedroom under its arching branches, and raised up their house around its strong trunk. This was the answer Penelope needed. It confirms her husband's identity, and it honours a key symbol of their life together. The living tree that forms their marital bed expresses the tough, durable strength of their union. Patiently hewn and sculpted by the hero, it harmoniously merges nature and art, solidity and grace, much like the well-wrought ships that long ago took the Greeks to Troy. The shared ordeals of husband and wife finally end here, far from the raging sea, in this living ark of their marriage.

It is often in this way, through the experience of suffering, that the European epic's courtship plots explore women's lives. In the Middle High German epic *Kudrun* (*c*.1250), one foreign prince after another invades King Hetel's realm to seize his beautiful daughter Kudrun as his bride. Battles abound, but the poem—often read as a critique of the revengeful *Nibelungenlied*—comes to focus on the patient resilience of women. Held captive for years by an obstinate suitor, shamefully abused by his sadistic mother, the princess is rescued at last when her own mother raises an army to liberate her. Kudrun promptly uses her political skills to fashion a web of dynastic marriages that reconcile the poem's warring factions and bring peace to their lands. Outside Europe too, marriage opens deep reservoirs of female suffering and heroism. African epic traditions teem with shrewd, resourceful women; many draw their power from close intimacy with the animal or spirit worlds. Among this sisterhood is Kumba, the hero's wife or consort in the Wassoulou *Epic of Kambili*. When her ex-lover, the lion man Cekura, terrorizes the village of Jimini, Kumba tricks him into giving her the secret tokens that Kambili needs to neutralize his occult power and destroy him. South Asian traditions can also give wives great spiritual agency. The widely beloved *Rāmāyaṇa*, for example, is a damsel-in-distress story: Rāma's wife Sītā, avatar of the goddess Lakshmī, follows him into exile in the Indian forests of Daṇḍaka and Panchavatī. When Sītā is abducted by the ten-headed Rāvaṇa, demon king of Lankā, Rāma must go to war against his *rākshasa* armies to rescue her. But Sītā does not droop like a wilting jasmine during her long captivity. She bravely resists Rāvana's lustful advances, and, after her liberation, when Rāma publicly doubts that his wife was faithful to him throughout her ordeal, she insists on a trial by fire to prove her constancy. In some versions of the tale, as Sītā walks unharmed across the burning coals, they miraculously turn into lotus flowers.

The fierce righteousness of abused women burns no less brightly in the *Cilappatikāram* ('the story of the anklet'), an ancient 5,700-line Tamil epic traditionally ascribed to Iḷaṅkō Aṭikaḷ, a probably fictitious Jain monk of the 2nd or 3rd century CE. The torments of Kaṇṇaki know no end. Her husband Kōvalaṉ abandons her for a courtesan and squanders their wealth. When he tires of the affair, Kaṇṇaki kindly takes him back, giving him a pair of her anklets to sell to a goldsmith. But the wicked goldsmith, who has stolen a similar anklet from the queen, accuses Kōvalaṉ of the crime. When Kaṇṇaki learns that the king has wrongly executed her husband, she storms into his palace and proves Kōvalaṉ's innocence before king and court. Cursing the kingdom, she rips off her left breast and flings it over the capital city, which burns to the ground. Escorted to heaven in Indra's chariot, she comes to be worshipped as Pattiṉi, the goddess of chastity. As a global art form, the epic is not merely a blood-soaked hunting ground for angry men. Its concern is the life of a community in all its complex moods and relations—a shared social experience tested and refined by heroic action under stress. Men and women are partners in the survival of their people, and the epic's ancient heritage belongs to them both.

Literary ancestors

Epics have families too. The world's epic traditions are shaped by the same dynamics of memory, inheritance, and rebellion that govern our family lives. Traditional storytellers are both rightful heirs and renegades, honouring their literary ancestry but also making it their own. Derek Walcott's *Omeros* (1990), for example, tells the story of a diverse community of fishermen, shopkeepers, and émigrés on his native island of St Lucia. Achille and Hector quarrel over their mutual love of Helen. Their friend Philoctete longs to heal a festering leg wound that has left him unemployed, drowning his sorrows in Ma Kilman's bar. Major Plunkett, scarred by the trauma of World War II and haunted by his failure to produce a son, devotes himself to researching the island's history while his neglected wife dies of cancer. All these stories bind the poem's characters to a global history. Their loves, their afflictions, and even their names evoke a far-reaching human story of intercultural contacts and conflicts: the Trojan War, the Conquistadors, the British Empire, the Middle Passage, global capitalism.

Also entangled in this vast story is the author's own biography. His father Warwick Walcott, a gifted painter who died when Derek was an infant, is the poem's Anchises. A spectre from the past, he rises before his son to issue two commands: the poet must travel far, touring the cultural capitals of Europe; but then, looking homeward, he must write the unsung story of his Caribbean birthplace and its people. Walcott's poem will stitch together a diverse heritage, one that includes the author's genetic inheritance from his artistic father; his bookish, multicultural boyhood; his poetry's ancestral ties to the European epic tradition; and the long, painful history of global violence, slavery, and colonialism that is etched into the lives and landscapes of the little West Indian island he calls home.

No epic is an orphan. Scholars of heroic literature often use biological metaphors: they suggest that epic traditions are organic, evolutionary, passing down family traits from one generation to the next. The old stories are reborn with each telling, introducing new genetic variations, but all bear family resemblances that mark their common ancestry in the tradition community. Heroes perish; bards falter and withdraw; but the story goes on, knitting and re-knitting the fibres of memory, patiently waiting to take new life in songs to come.

Chapter 6
Civilization and the wilderness

> He who saw the Deep, the country's foundation,
>> who knew the proper ways, was wise in all matters!

With its cryptic opening words, the *Epic of Gilgamesh* hails its hero as a restless seeker of wisdom. This prologue is a late addition to the poem, inserted by Babylonian scribes in the 1st millennium BCE. It portrays Gilgamesh as a sage who wrung knowledge from the cosmos, a man who 'saw what was secret, discovered what was hidden'. The prologue tells us two more things about this man: he travelled widely, and he built strong city walls.

> He came a far road, was weary, found peace,
>> All his labours were set on a tablet of stone.
> He built the rampart of Uruk-the-Sheepfold,
>> Of holy Eanna, the sacred storehouse.

Gilgamesh is an explorer with a lust for adventure, a boundary breaker. But he is also a civic leader, a boundary maker. The poem lingers over his city of Uruk, its sturdy fortifications, its groves of date trees, its glorious temple of Anu and Ishtar, the strength and splendour of the high walls that Gilgamesh built. Both roles shape Gilgamesh's heroic identity: he is a civilized nomad, a wanderer king.

Many epic heroes straddle the threshold, as Gilgamesh does, between civilization and the wilderness. An epic is a history book, but it is also a map. Environing the hero's community are foreign lands and peoples, exotic flora and fauna, occult energies, spirit realms. The hero moves out across that terrain in hopes of mastering its forces and widening the circle of the known. Epic heroes are made for large open spaces. They wander far from home and behold marvels. Yet when they stride into the wilderness, they rarely lose themselves to its strangeness. Still flickering inside them, like a candle in the dark, are memories of the homeland they have left behind. What makes epic heroes like Gilgamesh so well suited to carry that flame into the darkness is their unique double nature. They are partly mortal, partly divine, half domesticated, half wild. With their dual citizenship in the human and nonhuman worlds, they can reach across the great divide between self and other, between the known and the unknown.

Boundaries and border epics

Epic geography is crisscrossed by borders and thresholds. Borders are identity markers, conjuring communities into being by giving them a tangible outline. The wilderness that encircles a community both threatens and defines it. Human societies have always measured themselves against the strangers they see or imagine beyond their walls. Even nomadic peoples strongly identify themselves and their neighbours with the places where they dwell. Epic heroes who cross borders may find that they have stepped into another realm of existence, a funhouse world where the familiar forms of everyday life are warped and reconfigured. In the ancient epic traditions of India, for example, the forest often takes on this role, an otherworldly dominion beyond the known order of things. It is a place of pilgrimage, retreat, and exile, where kings fall in love with frog princesses, birds rear their young in nests built on the heads of meditating Brahmins, and heroes discuss the finer points of Dharma with talking snakes. Beyond the border, life operates under different laws.

And yet even distorting mirrors can show us our own reflection. Epics frequently set their scene at the contested border between two rival ethnic groups, in that shadowy no man's land where identity and difference struggle for mastery. Many of these border epics imagine neighbouring peoples as a monstrous caricature of the epic hero's own community. The hero's righteous violence, for example, might see its warped mirror image in the enemy's fanatical brutality. But a xenophobic ideology often cannot hide deeper forms of likeness and reciprocity that spill across borders. Indeed, it is hard to find any trace of ethnic chauvinism in the *Digenes Akritis*, a Greek epic romance that was perhaps compiled in the 12th century CE but takes place some two centuries earlier. Its setting is the eastern frontier of the Byzantine Empire. The poem has deep roots in the region's traditional acritic songs, which made folk heroes of the frontier guards (known as *aktritai*) who defended the empire's borderlands against relentless Muslim Arab invasions. What makes this poem so startling is how the hero's own identity knits together those two rival cultures. The poem tells how his father, an Arab emir, converted to Christianity for love of his Greek wife, whom he had abducted during a raid into Cappadocia. Their son's nickname honours his dual heritage: Digenes Akritis means 'two-blooded frontiersman' or 'double-born borderer'. Patrolling the eastern Anatolian fringes of the empire, he has no interest in holy war. To the contrary, his primary targets are Greek bandits who threaten the region's intercultural trade routes. Near the end of the poem, Digenes builds a shining palace for himself by the Euphrates River—an apt resting place for a man who seems most fully at home in the fertile, riverine folds of Asia Minor, with its hybrid ethnicities and plural allegiances.

Identity is just as fluid in the *Cantar de mío Cid*, an anonymous 3,730-line Spanish epic probably composed around 1200 CE and preserved in a damaged 14th-century manuscript. Its hero is the real-life Castilian warrior Rodrigo Díaz de Vivar. The poem portrays him as a loyal vassal of his Castilian king and a spearpoint of the Christian Reconquista. Long celebrated as a Spanish national hero, he is a man of piety and honour whose sword conquers Valencia for King Alfonso VI and drives the Moors before him across Iberia. Yet his allegiances are not so clear cut. Having offended the king, Rodrigo has been banished from Castile. His attacks on Muslim Spain are an effort to rebuild his public standing. After his victories win back the king's favour, Rodrigo must fight a new battle in the courtroom, as his military campaigns against the Moors give way to an ugly legal dispute with his own disreputable sons-in-law. Meanwhile, misprized at home, the Cid forges surprising economic and political ties behind enemy lines, where he amasses personal wealth and makes alliances with local Muslim warlords. Even Rodrigo's popular title, *mío Cid*, derives from *Sayyidī*, 'My lord'—an Arabic honorific that seems to have clung more tightly to this border-dwelling hero than his Spanish sobriquet, *el campeador* (the champion). Epic heroes will always be half-strangers to their own peoples, since the wilderness is part of who they are.

Quest and homecoming

An epic hero's greatest trials lie beyond these well-travelled borderlands. Among the best known of all epic story forms is, of course, the quest. Whether to seek or recover something of value, to confront a foreign threat, or simply to win fame, the hero must leave the community and set forth into the unknown. The journey might lead to the cedar forest of Humbaba, or the underwater lair of Grendel's mother, or the staging grounds of a new empire in Rome or Jerusalem. Many epic heroes begin their careers in exile: Manas, David of Sassoun, Zāl, Sunjata, Aeneas, El Cid, Rāma, and the Pāṇḍava brothers are just a few of these. Lost, orphaned, banished, or held in captivity, they inhabit the wilderness as castaways, outcasts, and émigrés, learning its secret ways even as they scheme to get back home or to create a new one.

It is a curious feature of early maps that the traveller who moves outward from the centre meets with ever wilder forms of life. Humanity seems to deform and mutate as its distance from home increases. Many epic landscapes follow the same uncanny logic. Gods and monsters dwell across the sea or over the next hill. Such is the world of the *Rāmāyaṇa*, a quest epic first written down in India during the 4th century CE but immensely popular throughout South Asia in its endless variants and adaptations. The troubles of Rāma and his wife Sītā, human incarnations of the Hindu gods Vishṇu and Lakshmī, thrust them deeper and deeper into the wilderness—first when Rāma's stepmother schemes to exile him to the forest for fourteen years; once again when Rāvaṇa, the demon king, kidnaps Sītā and carries her off to his island of Lankā; and yet once more when Rāma must visit Kiṣkindhā, homeland of the celestial monkeys known as Vānaras, to build an alliance for a great war against Rāvaṇa (see Figure 5). In these ever more alien climes, heroism is the struggle to know who you are and what you value most when all the external props and guarantors of selfhood have been left behind. It is telling that epic heroes often face enemies who, like Homer's Lotus-Eaters, would use drugs or spells to erase their memories or make them lose their longing for home.

The journey into the wilderness can sometimes be understood as a quest of initiation. The hero steps outside the familiar sphere, experiences growth and transformation, and then, having attained a new kind of selfhood, is reincorporated into the community, like Dorothy in *The Wizard of Oz*. A common symbol for this process is the stripping of the hero's clothing, as when Odysseus washes ashore naked in the land of Scheria, or when Rāma, exiled from his glittering capital city of Ayodhyā, exchanges his royal robes for crude garments made from tree-bark fibres. We must not push such readings too far. Traditional epic

5. Rāma and his brother Lakṣmaṇa (right) are distraught over the abduction of Sītā (left), from the 'Shangri' *Ramayana*, c.1700–1710.

heroes are not formless blobs waiting to be moulded into shape by their experiences, like the protagonists of certain Victorian novels. They are always fully themselves. Yet the hero's identity gains strength and clarity by experiencing other forms of being, by absorbing some of their essence without losing itself to them. In this sense, wherever the hero's path leads, it is also a voyage home.

The hero's homeward journey is a favourite epic theme in many cultures—most of all, perhaps, in the tightly interlaced oral storytelling traditions that stretch from the Balkans to the Altai Mountains of Kazakhstan. One of the most widespread story patterns in this region is the *return song*. A man leaves his homeland for several years, often languishing in captivity abroad, and is presumed dead. In his absence, a rival tries to seize his possessions and marry his wife or fiancée. The man finds his way home, typically disguising himself to test the loyalty of old friends and servants. At last, he takes revenge on the rival suitor and reunites with his bride. In this plot summary we might see the familiar outlines of Homer's *Odyssey*. But versions of the story have been collected all over Central Asia: for example, the traditional epic of *Alpamyš*, widely performed by the Uzbek, Kazakh, Karakalpak, and other Turkic singers known as *dastanči*. Another version, which includes an Odyssean archery contest, appears in the *Book of Dede Korkut*, a sprawling Turkic epic cycle that was first set down in writing in the 14th century CE. South Slavic oral traditions also abound with return songs. Hundreds have been collected in Bosnia and Croatia, including variants in which the hero learns that his wife has been unfaithful and kills her. These stories offer a tantalizing glimpse of vast networks of oral transmission that must have extended across Eurasia for more than 2,500 years.

The Homeric *Odyssey*, like those later return songs, shows that the hero's struggle to get home is more than a perilous trek across a map. It can also be a quest to gather and reassemble the broken pieces of the hero's identity. Odysseus is only one of several Greek war heroes whose legendary *nostoi*, or returns to their homelands after the Trojan War, were sung in the epic cycles of archaic Greece. For these tough old warriors, the path leading home is also a journey through time. The world has changed since they set sail for Troy twenty years before. That glorious heroic age is now ebbing away. The *Odyssey* often glances at the *nostoi* of Odysseus' companions on the battlefield—Menelaus, Nestor, Agamemnon—who must now squeeze themselves once more into civilized domestic spaces. Sitting in their Mycenaean palaces, they struggle to relearn the intricate codes of marriage and household government. This new world is both smaller and larger than the one they knew on the beaches of Troy.

To reach Ithaca, Odysseus must cross the sea. Its formless waters symbolize the threat that he will lose his own selfhood, or has already lost it, in the wilderness where he has sojourned for so long. When the story begins, Odysseus has been stranded for seven years, living with a sea nymph at the edge of the world. She is called

Calypso, from the Greek verb *kalyptein*, to cover or conceal, as if to warn the hero that his own famous name is fading from human memory while he lingers in her arms. Odysseus will recover his name only through hardship and suffering. In fact, suffering is Odysseus' name: the obscure verb *odyssasthai* in Homeric poetry means to be angry or to inflict pain. The cruel gods have odysseused Odysseus, and it is through pain—the pain he endures, the pain he inflicts—that he will become Odysseus once again. Rejecting Calypso's dream life of immortality, Odysseus chooses to return to a world of strife, heartbreak, and death, to restore an identity that can only be forged and reforged in woe.

When the *Odyssey* was composed in the 8th or 7th century BCE, the Greek world was rapidly expanding. Technical advances in shipbuilding and seamanship enabled far-reaching maritime travel. Greek merchants exchanged goods at foreign ports around the Adriatic Sea and far along the Mediterranean coastline. They imported textiles from Carthage, sails from Egypt, and incense from Syria. Foreign visitors exposed Greek craftsmen to new advances in metalworking and jewellery making. Hundreds of miles from their homeland, Greek colonists founded settlements encircling the Black Sea, dotting the shores of southern Italy and North Africa, and later reaching as far west as coastal France and Spain. The *Odyssey* arose from this Mediterranean culture of seaborne trade and colonization.

The poem describes Odysseus as a man who has travelled far and seen many cities, and his wanderings force him to come to grips with this strange new world. In the middle books, he makes contact with two overseas peoples who descend from the sea god Poseidon: the supremely civilized Phaeacians and the monstrous Cyclopes. The Phaeacians are technologically sophisticated, wealthy, and refined, a utopian society rich in art and culture. Their distant cousins, the Cyclopes, are crude and barbarous loners, lawless pastoralists who grow no crops and build no ships. Revealingly, the poem's key contrast between these two peoples is their treatment of outsiders. Hospitality is a core theme of the *Odyssey*, anchored in the powerful custom of *xenia* or guest-friendship: a framework of mutual obligations that governs the relationship between host and guest in the ancient Greek world. When the shipwrecked stranger washes up naked on the Phaeacians' shore, they feed and dress him, kindly invite him to take part in their aristocratic culture of storytelling and gift exchange, and provide safe passage to Ithaca on their fast ships. The Cyclopes, for their part, are shockingly inhospitable. Odysseus is eager to find out whether they will offer him guest gifts. Instead, Polyphemus imprisons Odysseus and his crewmates in his filthy cave and dines on his own guests. These encounters help to refine the hero's identity. He sees his own cultural heritage with new eyes when he measures it against the customs of these exotic peoples, far from home in the engulfing sea.

Descent to the underworld

As stories of all things, epic traditions place their heroes at the centre of a comprehensive world picture. In most human societies, the landscape of experience has a vertical dimension as well as a horizontal one. Our material plane intersects with a higher domain where gods, spirits, demons, and magical powers hold sway. This means that the epic is not just a map but a cosmology. In the wilderness, the hero encounters both the natural world and the supernatural realm, both the earthly and unearthly forces that govern human life.

Epic journeys rarely involve spaceflight, although the world's epic traditions do include a smattering of flying steeds, airborne sorcerers, angelic warriors, celestial chariots, and cosmic battles. Sometimes the hero rises above the earth in a dream vision. More commonly, the hero's path leads downward into the land of the dead. Many cultures tell stories about the underworld journeys of gods or exceptional mortals. Often called a *katabasis* (a Greek term for descent), the motif takes countless forms. The earliest known example dates back to the 21st century BCE, a Sumerian poem about the descent of Gilgamesh's friend Enkidu into the netherworld. Later variations on the theme include the myth of Orpheus and Euridice; the underworld trials of the twins Hunahpii and Xbalanqúe in the Mayan *Popol Vuh*; the god Izanagi's descent to Yomi in the Japanese *Kojiki*; and Christ's harrowing of hell. The goal of these heroic descents is usually to acquire a quest object or to bring a loved one back to life.

In the European epic tradition, the hero visits the underworld in search of secret knowledge that only the dead possess. Homer's Odysseus is the first of these wisdom seekers, sailing to the gates of Hades to ask the dead prophet Teiresias how he can get home to Ithaca. The Greeks labelled this episode the *nekuia* or summoning of ghosts. Many more heroes were to follow in Odysseus' footsteps. Each voyage has its own macabre rites to mark the unnatural crossing into death's kingdom: solemn prayers, sacrificial offerings, mystical talismans (such as the *Aeneid*'s famous golden bough), and the ministrations of shamanic guides to ensure safe passage. The signs are everywhere that the hero has crossed an awful threshold which no living being should trespass. Odysseus watches his dead mother drink the blood of a sacrificial sheep. When Virgil's Aeneas steps into Charon's boat to cross the Styx, the vessel groans and takes on water under the unaccustomed weight of flesh and blood.

To encounter the dead is to gaze into past times. In the underworld, the hero meets with throngs of lost friends and loved ones. There is a dismal poignancy in these reunions, always fleeting and incomplete. Odysseus tries three times to embrace his mother Anticlea, but he clutches empty air. The shades of the dead are imprisoned in the past. Their stories have ended. Some of them still seethe with anger and regret, nursing grudges over old wrongs that cannot be undone. Tearfully, Aeneas tries to mollify his abandoned lover Dido, but her phantom sullenly withdraws into the darkness. In these encounters the hero walks backward in pain through his own biography, recalls his missteps and failures, and counts his many losses. Reaching out in vain to those he loves, he feels his heroic isolation more deeply than ever, and his helplessness before the cruel majesty of death.

But all has not been lost. The netherworld, where the ancestors dwell, is a place of memory. When epic heroes speak with the dead, they gain access to their collective knowledge, patiently gathered over many generations. Here the story of their people merges with the hero's own. We can read the epic hero's katabasis as a metaphor for the relationship between the living and the dead that is culture itself. The epic underworld has sometimes been compared to the unconscious mind, preserving old myths and memories that might have been repressed or forgotten. These episodes also allow the epic to ponder its own literary ancestry—for what is an epic tradition but a dialogue with the dead?

In Virgil's *Aeneid* and many of its Western heirs, the epic hero who braves the underworld obtains a prophecy of the future. The hero learns about a perilous journey to come, or the illustrious descendants who will spring from his blood, or the great empires they will sow. More than just forecasts of upcoming events, these prophecies lay bare the secret workings of history. They grant the hero a rare glimpse of a higher design that shapes human action, the hidden hand of fate, the supervening will of the gods. The katabasis is therefore a crucial inflexion point, a communion with the past that equips the hero to face the future. This will be the remotest point on the outward voyage; the hero will never be further from home. But the deeper wisdom learned here reaffirms the hero's bonds with family, community, and history, and thus makes homecoming possible. In this way, we might understand the hero's descent to the underworld as a symbolic death and rebirth. The being who rises out of the darkness has been changed by this sojourn with the ancestors. Infused with their knowledge, the hero can now give them a new life.

The gods in epic

For all their fantastical wanderings, epics are human-centred stories. The wranglings of the gods more properly belong to myth. Still, traditional epic heroes nearly always contend with divine beings or magical energies as they pursue their goals. The role of the supernatural in the world's epics is hugely varied and complex, but one of its key attractions is its explanatory power. It draws back the curtain to expose the hidden scaffolding of the cosmos. The secret machinations of the gods—often disclosed to us in a *concilium deorum*, a sort of celestial cabinet meeting—give form and meaning to the muddle of history. Human affairs are shaped by divine agents whose motives, whether good or evil, can at least be understood. A community suffers because one of its members has offended a god or earned a shaman's curse. Forms of human behaviour that might seem irrational or wrongheaded can be blamed on the influence of higher beings. Some epic villains, for example, are demons incarnated in human flesh. Others have been possessed by gods who want to thwart the hero's cause.

Polytheistic religions lend themselves easily to this kind of storytelling. The gods are partisan actors, meddling in worldly conflicts that serve as proxies for their own divine quarrels. They take sides, form alliances, squabble, cheat, betray, lobby one another, and descend to earth to aid their human protégés. In some cultural traditions, epic heroes lose their independent life and become symbols for the cosmic forces that swirl and clash around them. One Middle Babylonian fragment of the *Epic of Gilgamesh*, for instance, mysteriously replaces the names of Gilgamesh and his friend Enkidu with those of Sîn, god of the moon and patron deity of Ur, and Ea, the mischievous water god. It seems that one group of ancient readers, at least, interpreted Gilgamesh's story as a cosmological allegory, revealing deeper truths about the nature of the universe.

When divine beings pry into the epic hero's concerns, they show that human life has dignity and importance. Humanity does not cower alone in a silent, uncaring cosmos. Epic heroes slam themselves against the boundaries of their mortal existence and force the gods to take notice of them. But the involvement of gods or spirits in worldly affairs also poses difficult questions about human freedom. Halfway through Virgil's *Aeneid*, the goddess Juno summons a Fury, Allecto, from her hellish lair to visit the sleeping Turnus, a rival suitor for Aeneas' Latin bride. The Fury's mission is to infect Turnus with febrile rage against the Trojan refugee:

> 'See what I've brought. I have come from the realm of
>   the Sisters of Terror,
> I decide wars, and death, with my own hand.'
> This said, she pointed a flaming brand at the youth and implanted
> Smoke-darkened light in his heart, the torches of death and
>   of marriage.
> Frightful and massive shock bursts in on his sleep, and erupting
> Sweat from his whole body drenches him through to his bones
>   and tendons.
> Mindlessly screaming for arms, he hunts arms in his chamber
>   and palace.

How should we understand this episode? Is it just an artful way for the poet to express Turnus' own hot-headedness? Many of Virgil's imitators thought so. Replaying this dream vision over and over in their own epics, they often simplified the forces at work by giving their Furies allegorical names like Envy or Cruelty. Or is this a genuine partnership between divine and human agency? Has Juno, sensing a kindred spirit in the Rutulian warrior, awakened passions that already slumbered within him? Or do these appalling images of possession and madness show that Juno has robbed Turnus of his free will, making him a helpless plaything of the vengeful goddess? If so, what responsibility does Turnus bear for waging war against Aeneas? Might those questions yield different answers in a Christian epic? What happens, for example, when Marco Girolamo Vida's *Christiad* (1535), an influential neo-Latin epic about the life of Jesus, replaces Juno and Turnus with Satan and Judas Iscariot? Episodes like these put intense pressure on the workings of human liberty in a cosmos ruled by supernatural forces.

Divine agents also raise unsettling questions about the nature of justice. In ancient cultures across Eurasia, one of the strangest and most moving aspects of epic storytelling is its double vision of the gods. They are flawed, fickle, and often cruel. They succumb to lust and anger. They hold grudges. They feel indignant, even anxious, when mortals reach up to challenge their power. Yet the traditional epic still honours them with reverence. Even as the bards take a clear-eyed view of the gods' inconstant ways, they nonetheless stand in awe of their divine power, and they submit without complaint to a cosmic hierarchy that calls on humanity to worship these capricious beings.

Divine justice is an even thornier problem for the world's monotheistic religions. In medieval and early modern Europe, flocks of would-be Virgils rushed to lay their own *Aeneids* on the altar of the Christian God. These poets sang of biblical heroes, saints' lives, and holy wars. What doomed so many of their epic poems to failure was the challenge of basing a meaningful human story on the premise of divine omnipotence. What interest lies in the trials of an epic hero sponsored by infinite power? What could drive the hero's enemies to take arms against an almighty being? If the hero's cause should falter, then why does God allow his champion to suffer? A perfectly just God would make the epic hero's task superfluous; an unjust God would make it intolerable.

Whether just or unjust, benign or wicked, the gods in epic embody raw power. Their desire to involve themselves in our endeavours gives dignity to human life, but we should not confuse dignity with pride. The gods' looming presence reminds us that victory depends on greater forces than the hero's will alone. Beyond all the other roles they play in the traditional epic, divine beings exist to patrol the borders of our mortal existence. When the hero quarrels with the conditions of human life, it is these beings who personify and enforce them. If the epic's supernatural agents were not there to block the hero's path, it might lead to godhead. The spirits, genies, nymphs, gods, and demons who twirl about the vertical axis of these epic worlds help to gauge the full scope of our aspirations, but they also remind us that humanity's reach will always exceed its grasp.

Taming the wilderness

Within the limits set by the gods, there is still a wide world to conquer. In Western thought, the wilderness is a nonhuman zone where animals and supernatural beings dwell. But all too often, this idea has also come to include foreign peoples living in faraway lands, whether real or imaginary. Some of these were believed to hover at the outer edges of humanity: Amazons, giants, pygmies, cannibals. For epic poets, these figures embodied powerful social taboos. Fearsome but strangely alluring, they lived at the margins of the human because they blurred identity categories. Their existence flouted age-old protocols that distinguished men from women or regulated what may and may not be eaten. To be civilized, in epic poetry from Virgil to Milton, was to draw dividing lines. Beyond those barricades lay the wild, the primitive, a realm of indistinction and boundary panic. Technological progress in medieval and early modern Europe further ordered and harnessed the known world, and only strengthened the instinct to view those outside its orbit as less than fully human.

This orbit widened in the 15th and 16th centuries with Europe's growing mastery over the world's oceans. The sea itself was an awesome wilderness, sometimes portrayed in epic literature as a primeval, chaotic force hostile to life. In ancient Greek mythology, the building of the first seagoing ships marked the end of the golden age. Maritime travel to unknown shores brought a loss of innocence as humanity embarked on a new era of far-flung intercultural contacts. By tradition, the first of all ships was believed to be the Argo, which brought Jason and his companions to the Black Sea kingdom of Colchis in their quest for the Golden Fleece. In the age of European colonial expansion, epic poets fashioned their own heroic tales of New World exploration and conquest. Columbus' voyages alone inspired dozens of epic poems, from Giovanni Giorgini's *Il Mondo Nuovo* (1596) to Joel Barlow's mystical *Columbiad* (1807). For readers back home, the colonists who cut their way across Africa and the Americas were at once like Jason, Aeneas, and Roland, expanding the sacred circle of civilization ever further into the wildlands.

Yet epic poets struggled to impose those ancient models of imperial geography onto the vast cultural diversity, strife, and suffering to which Europe's colonial project bore witness. A fascinating example is *La Araucana* (1569–89), an epic poem about the brutal Arauco War between colonial Spanish forces and the Mapuche people of southern Chile. Its author, Alonso de Ercilla y Zúñiga, who personally fought in the war, brought eyewitness realism to his portrayal of the conflict. His poem is striking for its frank admiration of the Mapuche's nobility of spirit, their courage under fire, and their arduous fight for freedom against his own Spanish army.

Europe's colonial activity in South Asia proved even harder to glorify. Luís de Camões, the great Portuguese poet-adventurer, wrote his epic *Os Lusíadas* (1572) during several years of military and diplomatic service in the Indian Ocean region. His poem portrays Vasco da Gama's pathbreaking sea voyages to India in

1497–8. Camões hails the Portuguese as the second Argonauts. They are the founders of a greater Roman Empire. Gama is a new Alexander, bringing another Persia under the Western yoke. But this was not a tale of New World conquest. Negotiating a commercial treaty with the Samorin of Calicut, Vasco da Gama only wanted to insert Portuguese merchants into a centuries-old Indian Ocean trading network. The poem's most haunting moments are those that expose the Europeans as latecomers and trespassers in this neighbourhood of old civilizations. As Gama's crew sets forth from Lisbon, an old man watches them from the harbour. Lamenting their quest for riches overseas, he bitterly curses the pride and avarice of the first shipbuilders. Later, amid the terrifying storms that torment the mariners at the Cape of Good Hope, they come upon an ancient titan of the seas who rebukes Gama for prying into the secrets of the deep. These are the voices of the old ones, the lost, the dispossessed. They do not stop the march of empire, but they will not let its victims be forgotten.

If the building of ships ended the golden age, it also affirmed humanity's dominion over the wilderness. Seafaring epics love to dwell on the skilful work of the shipwrights, the hewing of timbers, the fastening and caulking of plank boards, the hoisting of sails. Epic poets generally delight in portraying art and artistry of all kinds—an ornamental garden, an intricately engraved shield—which often serve as symbols for their own art of storytelling. A related cluster of images, found in epics all over the world, involves razing forests or cutting down trees. These woodlands are often imbued with a magical or divine taboo, as if hacking and burning our human signature onto the landscape comes with an uneasy feeling of desecration. Gilgamesh boldly undertakes to fell a cedar forest sacred to the gods, and to slay the ogre, Humbaba, who guards it. The *Mahābhārata*'s Arjuna and Krishna help the god Agni raze the Khāṇḍava forest and massacre its creatures, clearing the site that later becomes the Pandavas' capital city, Indraprashtha. In the Bamana epic *Sonsan of Kaarta*, the founder-hero Sonsan is instructed by a genie to cut down a sacred grove so that he can build the village of Sonsana. The Christian knights in Torquato Tasso's crusader epic *Gerusalemme Liberata* must tear down a grove haunted by demonic sorcery in order to supply timber for the siege machines they will use to conquer Jerusalem. With sword, axe, and fire, these epics assert the violent triumph of the human will over the natural environment.

How ironic, then, that epic heroes who would tame the wilderness also carry it within themselves. We noted earlier that the hero has a dual identity, both civilized and wild. This might be why so many epics are drawn to the folkloric figure of the wild man. These creatures are sometimes the hero's companions and helpers, from Gilgamesh's shaggy friend Enkidu to the Salvage Man in Spenser's *Faerie Queene*. The epic hero can also become feral, but it is nearly always a temporary condition: a princeling, abandoned in infancy, comes of age in the wilderness, like the hero of the Middle High German epic *Wolfdietrich*; or a lovestruck knight, driven mad by jealousy, strips off his clothes and goes crashing into the forest, as in Ariosto's *Orlando Furioso*. Still, something within the epic hero's nature feels most at home in wild places, alone and free. Over time, Western societies have slowly given up the search for wild men in distant lands. Modern psychology has instead found them living in our own hearts, in the bestial and anarchic drives that roil our consciousness. Self and community are always at risk of self-destruction—a widespread theme in world epic. Standing for civilization, the epic celebrates the use of artful and controlled aggression to beat back the wilderness. Yet its heroes, taking their ease in the palace or the mead hall, know that the wild man within is still untamed.

Chapter 7
Epic and modernity

The epic literature surveyed by this book has struggled to survive in the modern world. The Western epic tradition—the practice of writing long heroic poems modelled on Homer and Virgil—was clinging to life by the mid-19th century and all but dead by World War I. Many forces caused its demise. The horrors of mass warfare shattered the poets' fantasies of heroic violence. Scientific rationalism banished the epic's supernatural wonders. An information revolution spawned a literate, urban merchant class who cared little for stories about the long-dead ancestors of their social betters. Something else was changing too: a growing historical consciousness in the modern West. 'Is the *Iliad* at all compatible with the printing press and steam press?' asked Karl Marx. Enlightenment thinkers formed a concept of the progress of human civilization over time, powered by advances in science and technology, which brought a new sense of estrangement from the past.

Most premodern criticism of the epic, from Aristotle's *Poetics* to Dryden and Boileau, had focused on technical matters of structure and style. How many subplots are permissible? How should a hero talk? This was a great age of literary imitation, obsessed with cosmetic details that a skilful poet could learn to reproduce through the careful study of exemplary texts. In the 16th and 17th centuries, especially in Italy and France, this formalist approach hardened into strict rules for imitating the Greco-Roman epics: an often scolding, pedantic dogma which Alexander Pope mocked as 'A Receipt to Make an Epic Poem'. Bookstands groaned under growing stacks of neoclassical epics all over Europe, but most of these were little more than mechanical exercises, doggedly applying the dictates of the critical theorists. Pope could see that all this policing of literary form was really an effort to hide a creeping sense of disillusionment, a loss of appetite for blood and glory. Nearly everyone agreed that epic poetry was a didactic tool, its heroes modelling virtuous conduct for social elites. But what could Achilles teach a high society that fancied lapdogs and *billets-doux*? It was this mounting tension between the hallowed *form* of ancient heroic poetry and its outmoded *content* that gave rise to the European mock epic, which wittily dressed up the everyday business of modern life in a grandiloquent epic style. Although Pope himself had translated the Homeric epics, he tried and failed to write his own heroic poem about Brutus, the legendary founder of Britain; instead, he gave us *The Rape of the Lock* and *The Dunciad*.

The formalists argued that their canons of taste were universal laws, grounded in human nature, binding always and everywhere. Yet a new awareness of historical change began to infuse Western literary scholarship. Readers' eyes turned from the civilized Virgil to the archaic Homer. The epic poems of Homeric Greece came to seem primitive and wild—not timeless classics etched in eternity, but crude artifacts from the rough and tumble childhood of the human race. Romantic thought leaders from Rousseau to Goethe imagined the archaic Greeks as a naive, dreamy nation, ardent, close to nature, whose life itself was poetry. G. W. F. Hegel argued that epics like the *Iliad* and *Odyssey* took shape at a time when the human spirit throbbed in unison with the outside world, when the mind embraced the totality of experience without questioning or doubt. Nations had not yet learned to express their shared identity through laws, civil institutions, or religious doctrines. Instead, people somehow poured the essence of their national character into heroic songs. Epic poetry, in other words, was not a bundle of stylistic conventions; it was a lost way of life, a fleeting dream of unity and belonging, the voice of a people wholly at home in their world.

For the Hegelians, this dream ended when we awoke into modernity. A new literary form, the novel, would now speak for our homeless age. In his *Theory of the Novel* (1916), the Marxist literary critic Georg Lukács argued that the rise of the novel marked the loss of humanity's primitive wholeness of being. The ancient epics had portrayed a tightly integrated lifeworld, saturated with meaning, where human consciousness was at one with the objective existence outside the self. But today's artists could no longer grasp the totality of life because the modern mind had retreated into itself, alienated from the world it once called home. 'The novel', Lukács wrote, 'is the epic of a world that has been abandoned by God.' Its primeval radiance has gone dark. Its heroes are lonely exiles, imprisoned in their own subjectivity, who can find meaning only within themselves.

If some modern intellectuals were nostalgic for the epic's holistic union of self and world, others cheered its collapse. In a series of essays written between 1934 and 1941 under the shadow of Joseph Stalin, the Russian philosopher Mikhail Bakhtin makes epic poetry look very much like a totalitarian state: repressive, hierarchical, univocal, bent on crushing dissent. The novel, for its part, is a plucky rebel, blasting apart the epic's closed world system and liberating its silenced voices. With its weaponry of dialogue and pluralism, the novel records the hubbub of social life in all its boisterous freedom. The epic can only remember an idealized past, forever cut off from the poet's own time; the novel, by contrast, is flexible, protean, centrifugal, open-ended, and always evolving to keep pace with a dynamic modern world. Whether the age of epic was a dream or a nightmare, many critics agreed that its distinctive vision of the human experience had long since vanished in the morning mist.

Yet the desire to create an all-embracing work of art lingered on, restlessly seeking new forms to fulfil itself. Some poets wrote translations of older epics. A few composed epic fictions that took place far away—in Europe's overseas colonies, for example—where primitive Homers might still be thought to warble their native woodnotes. Others found (or invented) oral epic traditions at the wild fringes of Europe itself, such as James Macpherson's *The Works of Ossian* (1765) and Elias Lönnrot's *Kalevala* (1849). Meanwhile, the crucial shift from formalism to historicism in Western thought gave writers the freedom to try out new epic forms, no longer constrained by neoclassical rules and templates. Now sprang up epic novels in verse, such as Elizabeth Barrett Browning's *Aurora Leigh* (1856); long visionary cycle poems like Victor Hugo's *La Légende des siècles* (1859–83); and the free-verse barbaric yawp that is Walt Whitman's *Song of Myself* (1855–92). Even stranger hybrid creations took life during these years, shapeless fictions that defied traditional labels, such as Johann Wolfgang von Goethe's *Faust* (1832), Herman Melville's *Moby-Dick* (1851), and Richard Wagner's *Der Ring des Nibelungen* (1874). Some scholars have called these modern epics. Vast in scope, still daring to transform history into myth, they were among the last great Western literary works that could aspire to be stories of all things.

The European epic tradition continued to haunt the imaginations of 20th-century modernists, but their responses to its legacy were experimental and fragmentary. The time for grand narratives was over. Smallness contends with greatness in James Joyce's *Ulysses* (1922), which transforms Homer's *Odyssey* into the meanderings of a middle-aged Jewish advertising agent in Dublin on 16 June 1904. Its story of homecoming takes shape in a miniature universe of daunting complexity; the author showed his friends various explanatory rubrics that laid out intricate correspondences linking the novel's chapters, related episodes in Homer, and archetypal symbols such as colours and body parts. But *Ulysses* is best remembered for the way it portrays something far from universal: a human being's unique stream of consciousness at a moment in time.

The poets, meanwhile, sifted through their cultural heritage to find scraps of old texts that might be recombined to make new art forms. T. S. Eliot's *The Waste Land* (1922) tries to bind up a wounded world with a patchwork of literary quotations—from the Bible, Ovid, Dante, Shakespeare, Baudelaire—interwoven with ancient fertility myths that portray the death and rebirth of an ailing god. Ezra Pound's *Cantos* (1930–59), a massive polyglot collage of global cultural traditions, draws on sources ranging from ancient Chinese chronicles to 18th-century American banking law; its opening lines quote Homer's Odysseus as he visits the gates of Hades to speak with the dead. All these 20th-century masterpieces grope toward new relationships between self, nation, and world under a modern sky. If epic heroes can be found in these texts, they are visionary nomads who drift alone through the wreckage of history, desert saints whose creed has no name.

In the post-war era, Western authors swept away the modernists' bric-a-brac of verbal allusions and turned to more radical kinds of adaptation and revision. In her lyric cycle *Helen in Egypt* (1961), the poet H.D. responds to Homer (and to her erstwhile lover, Ezra Pound) with an enigmatic portrait of Helen of Troy, whose mystical femininity scorns epic poetry's obsession with brutal men like Achilles:

> his fortress and his tower
> and his throne
> were built for man, alone;
>
> no echo or soft whisper
> in those halls,
> no iridescent sheen,

no iris-flower,

no sweep of strings,

no answering laughter,

but the trumpet's call;

does he still wait the dead,

to challenge the celestial hierarchy?

whose are the dead

and whose the victory?

Following in its wake were sensitive lyric meditations on the Homeric epics such as Christopher Logue's unfinished *War Music* (1981–2016) and Alice Oswald's *Memorial* (2011). But some of the richest engagements with the European epic tradition since the 1970s have come from novelists, eager to retell the old stories from new viewing angles. Questioning the epic's timeworn ideals, they ask us to look through the eyes of its villains, its victims, its silent witnesses. The monsters of *Beowulf* find their own voices in John Gardner's *Grendel* (1971) and Maria Dahvana Headley's *The Mere Wife* (2018). Madeline Miller brings to life the lovers and companions of the Homeric heroes in *The Song of Achilles* (2011) and *Circe* (2018). Pat Barker tells how the Greeks' wives and bondslaves bore the trauma of the Trojan War in *The Silence of the Girls* (2018) and *The Women of Troy* (2022). Ursula K. Le Guin's last novel, *Lavinia* (2008), reworks Virgil's *Aeneid* so that the Trojan hero's wordless bride can speak for herself at last. The patient wife of Odysseus tells her own tale of woe in Margaret Atwood's *Penelopiad* (2005)—but so, too, do her twelve maidservants, executed in cold blood by the homecoming hero. These novels honour the enduring power of the epic poems that inspired them. Yet the ghosts that haunt their fictions are those that the bards failed to perceive as we do: shadowy figures gliding through distant mists, keen eyes watching from the darkness.

Over the last century, the Western epic has splintered into so many cultural forms that it would be a hopeless task to survey them all.

There are mock-epic pastiches like Gwendolyn Brooks's 'The Anniad' (1949), mixed-media scrapbooks like William Carlos Williams's *Paterson* (1946–58), and huge amalgams of lyric poems on world-historical themes such as Pablo Neruda's *Canto General* (1950). Odyssean wandering is a favourite theme, as in Saint-John Perse's *Anabasis* (1924) and Nikos Kazantzakis's *Odysseia* (1938). Some scholars use the term *epic novel* to describe monumental prose fictions that trace the life of a clan or nation across space and time—think of John Steinbeck's *The Grapes of Wrath* (1939) or Salman Rushdie's *Midnight's Children* (1981). We might also look to the *episches Theater* of Bertolt Brecht, an activist political drama that tries to expose the scaffolding behind bourgeois theatrical illusions.

Or we might instead consider the epic film, a big-budget cinematic spectacle steeped in mythlike grandeur. Most closely associated with Hollywood's biblical and Roman blockbusters of the 1950s and 1960s, which upheld a conservative vision of American cultural identity at the height of the Cold War, the label has been more loosely applied to films as diverse as *Gone with the Wind* (1939), *Ben-Hur* (1959), *Apocalypse Now* (1979), and *Titanic* (1997). And then there are weighty world-building fictions in the realm of fantasy and science fiction, from J. R. R. Tolkien's *The Lord of the Rings* (1954–5) to George Lucas's Star Wars saga. These can either advance or challenge the Western epic tradition's great themes of territorial expansion and empire building, taking forms as diverse as Stanley Kubrick's fittingly named *2001: A Space Odyssey* (1968), Dan Simmons's novels *Ilium* (2003) and *Olympos* (2005), and James Cameron's *Avatar* (2009). This is to say nothing of dance, opera, painting, graphic novels, television series, or video games. But here we have drifted far from the six traits of the traditional epic that we considered in Chapter 1. The works listed above have little in common except their sheer bulk and their lofty artistic ambitions.

As for the ancient formal features of the Greco-Roman epics, they linger now mostly in literary satire. 'Hail, Muse! et cetera,' smirked

Lord Byron in *Don Juan*. The textbook definition of the epic that opened our Chapter 1, with its dactylic hexameter and *in medias res*, describes a literary form that no longer exists. Nor has its ideology aged much better than its style. Modern readers criticize the Western epic tradition for its conservative social vision. They shrink from its glorification of violence and power. They reject its ethnic chauvinism and constricted gender roles. Yet the epic poems of Homer and Virgil and Milton still matter today because they ponder certain aspects of the human experience more deeply than any other art form. These are stories about life *in extremis*. They show us the human spirit under stress, testing its limits in adversity. Many of us feel a kind of awe in watching epic heroes dig in their heels and make the universe yield to their demands. No other literary form is so much in love with humanity's inborn potential for greatness. None is so keenly aware of the pain it brings.

The epic still matters, too, for what we might call its global outlook. Long before the rise of modern nation states, epic singers taught their communities to view themselves as world citizens, vital participants in a shared human story. They sang of war, migration, and intercultural exchange in a cosmos teeming with interdependent life. This book has argued that the epic is a global art form in another sense as well. Many indigenous storytelling traditions around the world resemble the heroic poetry of premodern Europe. These also deserve the prestigious name of epic. In their endless diversity, they display an astonishing capacity to adapt and renew themselves over time. So the epic lives on, but not always where we might expect to find it: in a *Manas* television serial in Kyrgyzstan, perhaps, or a staging of the *Rāmāyaṇa* in a Balinese puppet theatre. Its formal designs will keep evolving, but its stories will persist. For we cannot help but dream of what humanity could be; nor can we forget the high cost of our ambitions.

References

Quotations in this book derive from the following sources; translations of primary sources not listed below are my own.

Barrett Browning, Elizabeth. *Aurora Leigh*, edited by Kerry McSweeney. Oxford: Oxford University Press, 1993, pp. 152–3.

Crossley-Holland, Kevin, trans. *Beowulf; The Fight at Finnsburh*. Oxford: Oxford University Press, 1999, pp. 4, 5.

George, Andrew, trans. *The Epic of Gilgamesh*, 2nd edn. New York: Penguin, 2020, p. 1.

H.D. [Hilda Doolittle]. *Helen in Egypt*. New York: New Directions, 1974, pp. 30–1.

Homer. *The Iliad*, translated by Anthony Verity. Oxford: Oxford University Press, 2011, pp. 3, 94, 322, 401.

Johnson, John William, Thomas A. Hale, and Stephen Belcher, eds. *Oral Epics from Africa: Vibrant Voices from a Vast Continent*. Bloomington: Indiana University Press, 1997, p. 105.

Lukács, Georg. *The Theory of the Novel*, translated by Anna Bostock. Cambridge: MIT Press, 1971, p. 88.

Lucan. *Civil War*, translated by Susan H. Braund. Oxford: Oxford University Press, 2008, p. 3.

Milton, John. *The Major Works*, edited by Stephen Orgel and Jonathan Goldberg. Oxford: Oxford University Press, 1991, pp. 363, 422–3, 483.

Philippi, Donald L. *Songs of Gods, Songs of Humans: The Epic Tradition of the Ainu*. Princeton: Princeton University Press, 1979, p. 328.

Sümer, Faruk, Ahmet E. Uysal, and Warren S. Walker, ed. and trans. *The Book of Dede Korkut: A Turkish Epic*. Austin: University of Texas Press, 1972, pp. 10–11.

Virgil. *The Aeneid*, translated by Frederick Ahl. Oxford: Oxford University Press, 2007, p. 172.

Zenkovsky, Serge A., ed. *Medieval Russia's Epics, Chronicles, and Tales*. New York: Penguin, 1974, p. 186.

Further reading

Comparative and world epic

Robert S. Auty and A. T. Hatto, eds., *Traditions of Heroic and Epic Poetry*, 2 vols. (Modern Humanities Research Association, 1980–9)

Margaret H. Beissinger, Jane Tylus, and Susanne Lindgren Wofford, eds., *Epic Traditions in the Contemporary World: The Poetics of Community* (University of California Press, 1999)

C. M. Bowra, *Heroic Poetry* (Macmillan, 1952)

Jeremy M. Downes, *The Female Homer: An Exploration of Women's Epic Poetry* (University of Delaware Press, 2010)

John Miles Foley, *Traditional Oral Epic: The Odyssey, Beowulf, and the Serbo-Croatian Return Song* (University of California Press, 1990)

Albert B. Lord, *The Singer of Tales*, 2nd edn., ed. by Stephen Mitchell and Gregory Nagy (Harvard University Press, 2000)

Albert Bates Lord, *Epic Singers and Oral Tradition* (Cornell University Press, 1991)

Dean A. Miller, *The Epic Hero* (Johns Hopkins University Press, 2000)

Felix J. Oinas, ed., *Heroic Epic and Saga: An Introduction to the World's Great Folk Epics* (Indiana University Press, 1978)

Karl Reichl, *The Oral Epic: From Performance to Interpretation* (Routledge, 2021)

Christiane Reitz and Simone Finkmann, eds., *Structures of Epic Poetry*, 4 vols. (De Gruyter, 2019)

Ancient Greece and Rome

D. C. Feeney, *The Gods in Epic: Poets and Critics of the Classical Tradition* (Oxford University Press, 1991)

John Miles Foley, ed., *A Companion to Ancient Epic* (Blackwell, 2005)

J. B. Hainsworth, *The Idea of Epic* (University of California Press, 1991)

Philip Hardie, *The Epic Successors of Virgil* (Cambridge University Press, 1993)

S. J. Harrison, ed., *Oxford Readings in Vergil's Aeneid* (Oxford University Press, 1990)

A. M. Keith, *Engendering Rome: Women in Latin Epic* (Cambridge University Press, 2000)

Katherine Callen King, *Ancient Epic* (Wiley-Blackwell, 2012)

G. S. Kirk, *The Songs of Homer* (Cambridge University Press, 1962)

Gregory Nagy, *The Ancient Greek Hero in 24 Hours: A New Edition* (Belknap, 2020)

Brooks Otis, *Virgil: A Study in Civilized Poetry* (Clarendon Press, 1964)

M. C. J. Putnam, *Virgil's Aeneid: Interpretation and Influence* (University of North Carolina Press, 1995)

Seth L. Schein, *The Mortal Hero: An Introduction to Homer's Iliad* (University of California Press, 1984)

Ruth Scodel, *Listening to Homer: Tradition, Narrative, and Audience* (Michigan University Press, 2009)

Peter Toohey, *Reading Epic: An Introduction to the Ancient Narratives* (Routledge, 1992)

European epic and heroic traditions

Catherine Bates, ed., *The Cambridge Companion to the Epic* (Cambridge University Press, 2010)

C. M. Bowra, *From Virgil to Milton* (Macmillan, 1945)

Colin Burrow, *Epic Romance: Homer to Milton* (Clarendon Press, 1993)

Robert M. Durling, *The Figure of the Poet in Renaissance Epic* (Harvard University Press, 1965)

Thomas M. Greene, *The Descent from Heaven: A Study in Epic Continuity* (Yale University Press, 1963)

Philip Hardie, *The Last Trojan Hero: A Cultural History of Virgil's Aeneid* (I. B. Tauris, 2014)

Edward R. Haymes and Susann T. Samples, *Heroic Legends of the North: An Introduction to the Nibelung and Dietrich Cycles* (Garland, 1996)

Catherine M. Jones, *An Introduction to the Chansons de Geste* (University Press of Florida, 2014)

John Kevin Newman, *The Classical Epic Tradition* (University of Wisconsin Press, 1986)

John D. Niles, *Beowulf: The Poem and Its Tradition* (Harvard University Press, 1983)

David Quint, *Epic and Empire: Politics and Generic Form from Virgil to Milton* (Princeton University Press, 1993)

William B. Stanford, *The Ulysses Theme: A Study in the Adaptability of a Traditional Hero*, 2nd edn. (Blackwell, 1968)

Mihoko Suzuki, *Metamorphoses of Helen: Authority, Difference, and the Epic* (Cornell University Press, 1989)

Africa

Ralph Austen, *In Search of Sunjata: The Mande Oral Epic as History, Literature and Performance* (Indiana University Press, 1999)

Stephen Belcher, *Epic Traditions of Africa* (Indiana University Press, 1999)

Daniel P. Biebuyck, *Hero and Chief: Epic Literature from the Banyanga (Zaire Republic)* (University of California Press, 1978)

Daniel Biebuyck and Kahombo C. Mateene, *The Mwindo Epic from the Banyanga* (University of California Press, 2021)

John William Johnson and Fa-Digi Sisòkò, *The Epic of Son-Jara: A West African Tradition* (Indiana University Press, 1986)

John William Johnson, Thomas A. Hale, and Stephen Belcher, eds., *Oral Epics from Africa: Vibrant Voices from a Vast Continent* (Indiana University Press, 1997)

Mugyabuso M. Mulokozi, *The African Epic Controversy: Historical, Philosophical, and Aesthetic Perspectives on Epic Poetry and Performance* (Mkuki Na Nyota, 2002)

Isidore Okpewho, *The Epic in Africa: Toward a Poetics of the Oral Performance* (Columbia University Press, 1979)

Jonathon Repinecz, *Subversive Traditions: Reinventing the West African Epic* (Michigan State University Press, 2019)

Central Asia and the Middle East

Nora K. Chadwick and Victor Zhirmunsky, *Oral Epics of Central Asia* (Cambridge University Press, 1969)

Bridget Connelly, *Arabic Folk Epic and Identity* (University of California Press, 1986)

Hamid Dabashi, *The Shahnameh: The Persian Epic as World Literature* (Columbia University Press, 2019)

David Damrosch, *The Buried Book: The Loss and Rediscovery of the Great Epic of Gilgamesh* (H. Holt, 2007)

Olga M. Davidson, *Poet and Hero in the Persian Book of Kings*, 3rd edn. (Harvard University Press, 2013)

B. R. Foster, ed. and trans., *The Epic of Gilgamesh* (W. W. Norton, 2000)

Chao Gejin, *Oral Epic Traditions in China and Beyond*, trans. by Liang Yanjun (Routledge, 2022)

M. C. Lyons, *The Arabian Epic: Heroic and Oral Story-Telling*, 3 vols. (Cambridge University Press, 1995)

Karl Reichl, *Turkic Oral Epic Poetry: Traditions, Forms, Poetic Structure* (Garland, 1992)

Dwight Fletcher Reynolds, *Heroic Poets, Poetic Heroes: The Ethnography of Performance in an Arabic Oral Epic Tradition* (Cornell University Press, 1995)

G. M. H. Shoolbraid, *The Oral Epic of Siberia and Central Asia* (Indiana University Press, 1975)

India and Southeast Asia

Brenda E. F. Beck, *The Three Twins: The Telling of a South Indian Folk Epic* (Indiana University Press, 1982)

Stuart H. Blackburn, Peter J. Claus, Joyce B. Flueckiger, and Susan S. Wadley, eds., *Oral Epics in India* (University of California Press, 1989)

Mandakranta Bose, ed., *The Rāmāyaṇa Revisited* (Oxford University Press, 2004)

John Brockington, *The Sanskrit Epics* (Brill, 1998)

Joyce Burkhalter Flueckiger and Laurie J. Sears, eds., *Boundaries of the Text: Epic Performances in South and Southeast Asia* (Center for South and Southeast Asian Studies, University of Michigan, 1991)

Lauri Honko, *Textualising the Siri Epic* (Academia Scientiarum Fennica, 1998)

K. Kailasapathy, *Tamil Heroic Poetry* (Clarendon, 1968)

Paula Richman, ed., *Many Rāmāyaṇas: The Diversity of a Narrative Tradition in South Asia* (University of California Press, 1991)

Gene H. Roghair, *The Epic of Palnāḍu* (Clarendon, 1982)

Barend A. Van Nooten, *The Mahābhārata* (Twayne, 1971)

Modern epic

Fiona Cox and Elena Theodorakopoulos, eds., *Homer's Daughters: Women's Responses to Homer in the Twentieth Century and Beyond* (Oxford University Press, 2019)

Robert D. Hamner, *Epic of the Dispossessed: Derek Walcott's Omeros* (University of Missouri Press, 1997)

Franco Moretti, *Modern Epic: The World-System from Goethe to García Márquez* (Verso, 1996)

Christopher N. Phillips, *Epic in American Culture: Settlement to Reconstruction* (Johns Hopkins University Press, 2012)

Sneharika Roy, *The Postcolonial Epic: From Melville to Walcott and Ghosh* (Routledge, 2018)

Constantine Santas, *The Epic in Film: From Myth to Blockbuster* (Rowman & Littlefield, 2008)

Bernard Schweizer, ed., *Approaches to the Anglo and American Female Epic, 1621–1982* (Ashgate, 2006)

Oliver Tearle, *The Great War, The Waste Land and the Modernist Long Poem* (Bloomsbury, 2019)

Herbert F. Tucker, *Epic: Britain's Heroic Muse 1790–1910* (Oxford University Press, 2008)

Thomas A. Vogler, *Preludes to Vision: The Epic Venture in Blake, Wordsworth, Keats and Hart Crane* (University of California Press, 1971)

Brian Wilkie, *Romantic Poets and Epic Tradition* (University of Wisconsin Press, 1965)

Further reading

Index

For the benefit of digital users, indexed terms that span two pages (e.g., 52–53) may, on occasion, appear on only one of those pages.

Index

The Epic

BESTSELLERS
A Very Short Introduction
John Sutherland

'I rejoice', said Doctor Johnson, 'to concur with the Common Reader.' For the last century, the tastes and preferences of the common reader have been reflected in the American and British bestseller lists, and this *Very Short Introduction* takes an engaging look through the lists to reveal what we have been reading - and why. John Sutherland shows that bestseller lists monitor one of the strongest pulses in modern literature and are therefore worthy of serious study. Along the way, he lifts the lid on the bestseller industry, examines what makes a book into a bestseller, and asks what separates bestsellers from canonical fiction.

'His amiable trawl through the history of popular books is frequently entertaining'

Scott Pack, The Times

BIOGRAPHY
A Very Short Introduction
Hermione Lee

Biography is one of the most popular, best-selling, and widely-read of literary genres. But why do certain people and historical events arouse so much interest? How can biographies be compared with history and works of fiction? Does a biography need to be true? Is it acceptable to omit or conceal things? Does the biographer need to personally know the subject? Must a biographer be subjective? In this *Very Short Introduction* Hermione Lee considers the cultural and historical background of different types of biographies, looking at the factors that affect biographers and whether there are different strategies, ethics, and principles required for writing about one person compared to another. She also considers contemporary biographical publications and considers what kind of 'lives' are the most popular and in demand.

'It would be hard to think of anyone better to provide a crisp contribution to OUP's Very Short Introductions.'

Kathryn Hughes, The Guardian

CHILDREN'S LITERATURE
A Very Short Introduction
Kimberley Reynolds

Children's literature is vast and amorphous subject. From picture books and pop ups, to online games and eBooks, children's literature takes many forms.

In this energetic *Very Short Introduction,* Kim Reynolds details what children's literature is, why it's interesting, how it contributes to culture, and how it is studied. Reynolds considers how children's literature has helped to shape and direct ideas about culture, society and childhood as well as exploring how far negative depictions of the future for children may contribute to a lack of social vision. She raises questions about what shape the future of literature for children should take, and explores the crossover between children's literature and adult fiction.

www.oup.com/vsi

COMEDY
A Very Short Introduction
Matthew Bevis

What is humour, and how may it be used (or abused)? When do we laugh, and why? What is it that writers and speakers enjoy—or risk—when they tell a joke, indulge in bathos, talk nonsense, or encourage irony?

This *Very Short Introduction* considers comedy not only as a literary genre, but also as a broader impulse at work in many other historical and contemporary forms of satire, parody, and play. Matthew Bevis takes us through the history of comedy, from the work of John Gay and Richard Sheridan in the eighteenth century to twentieth-century dramatists like Ionesco, Brecht and Cocteau, up to present day interpretations of comedy, such as Charlie Kaufman's *Being John Malkovich* and Channel 4's *Peep Show*.

www.oup.com/vsi

FAIRY TALE
A Very Short Introduction
Marina Warner

From wicked queens to goblins and giants, glass slippers to poisoned apples, the characters and images of fairy tales have cast a spell over readers for centuries. Few forms of literature have greater power to enchant us and rekindle our imagination than a fairy tale.

In this *Very Short Introduction*, Marina Warner digs into a rich hoard of fairy tales in all their brilliant and fantastical variations, in order to define a genre and evaluate a literary form that keeps shifting through time and history. Drawing on a glittering array of examples, from classics such as Red Riding Hood, Cinderella, and The Sleeping Beauty, to modern-day realizations including Walt Disney's *Snow White*, Warner forms a persuasive case for fairy tale as a crucial repository of human understanding and culture.

FILM
A Very Short Introduction
Michael Wood

Film is considered by some to be the most dominant art form
of the twentieth century. It is many things, but it has become
above all a means of telling stories through images and sounds.
The stories are often offered to us as quite false, frankly and
beautifully fantastic, and they are sometimes insistently said to
be true. But they are stories in both cases, and there are very
few films, even in avant-garde art, that don't imply or quietly slip
into narrative. This story element is important, and is closely
connected with the simplest fact about moving pictures: they
do move. In this *Very Short Introduction* Michael Wood provides
a brief history and examination of the nature of the medium of
film, considering its role and impact on society as well as its
future in the digital age.

FRENCH LITERATURE
A Very Short Introduction
John D. Lyons

The heritage of literature in the French language is rich,
varied, and extensive in time and space; appealing both to its
immediate public, readers of French, and also to aglobal
audience reached through translations and film adaptations.
French Literature: A Very Short Introduction introduces this lively
literary world by focusing on texts - epics, novels, plays, poems,
and screenplays - that concern protagonists whose adventures
and conflicts reveal shifts in literary and social practices. From
the hero of the medieval *Song of Roland* to the Caribbean
heroines of *Tituba, Black Witch of Salem* or the European
expatriate in Japan in *Fear and Trembling*, these problematic
protagonists allow us to understand what interests writers and
readers across the wide world of French.

www.oup.com/vsi

ROMANTICISM
A Very Short Introduction
Michael Ferber

What is Romanticism? In this *Very Short Introduction*
Michael Ferber answers this by considering who the romantics
were and looks at what they had in common – their ideas, beliefs,
commitments, and tastes. He looks at the birth and growth
of Romanticism throughout Europe and the Americas, and
examines various types of Romantic literature, music, painting,
religion, and philosophy. Focusing on topics, Ferber looks at the
rising prestige of the poet; Romanticism as a religious trend;
Romantic philosophy and science; Romantic responses to the
French Revolution; and the condition of women. Using examples
and quotations he presents a clear insight into this very diverse
movement.

www.oup.com/vsi

RUSSIAN LITERATURE
A Very Short Introduction
Catriona Kelly

Rather than a conventional chronology of Russian literature,
Catriona Kelly's *Very Short Introduction* explores the place and
importance of diverse literature in Russian culture. How and when
did a Russian national literature come into being? What shaped its
creation? How have the Russians regarded their literary language?
At the centre of the web is the figure of Pushkin, 'the Russian
Shakespeare', whose work influenced all Russian writers, whether
poets or novelists, and many great artists in other areas as well.

'brilliant and original, taking an unexpected approach to the
subject, and written with great confidence and clarity.'

Peter France, University of Edinburgh

'a great pleasure to read. It is a sophisticated, erudite, searching,
and subtle piece of work. It is written in a lively and stimulating
manner, and displays a range to which few of Dr Kelly's peers in
the field of Russian scholarship can aspire.'

**Phil Cavendish, School of Slavonic and
East European Studies, University of London**

SPANISH LITERATURE
A Very Short Introduction
Jo Labanyi

This *Very Short Introduction* explores the rich literary history of Spanish literature, which resonates with contemporary debates on transnationalism and cultural diversity. The book introduces a general readership to the ways in which Spanish literature has been read, in and outside Spain, explaining misconceptions, outlining the insights of recent scholarship and suggesting new readings. It highlights the precocious modernity of much early modern Spanish literature, and shows how the gap between modern ideas and social reality stimulated creative literary responses in subsequent periods; as well as how contemporary writers have adjusted to Spain's recent accelerated modernization.

GERMAN LITERATURE
A Very Short Introduction
Nicholas Boyle

German writers, from Luther and Goethe to Heine, Brecht, and Günter Grass, have had a profound influence on the modern world. This *Very Short Introduction* presents an engrossing tour of the course of German literature from the late Middle Ages to the present, focussing especially on the last 250 years. Emphasizing the economic and religious context of many masterpieces of German literature, it highlights how they can be interpreted as responses to social and political changes within an often violent and tragic history. The result is a new and clear perspective which illuminates the power of German literature and the German intellectual tradition, and its impact on the wider cultural world.

'Boyle has a sure touch and an obvious authority...this is a balanced and lively introduction to German literature.'

Ben Hutchinson, TLS

WILLIAM SHAKESPEARE
A Very Short Introduction
Stanley ells

In this new offering from Stanley Wells, the pre-eminent
Shakespearian scholar, comes an exploration of one of the
world's greatest dramatists: William Shakespeare.

Examining Shakespeare's narrative poems, sonnets, and all of his
plays, Wells outlines their sources, style, and originality over the
course of Shakespeare's career, to consider the fundamental
impact his work has had for subsequent generations. Written
with enthusiasm and flair by a scholar who has devoted a lifetime
to the study of Shakespeare and his works, this is an engaging
and authoritative introduction that looks at both the world
Shakespeare lived in and all of his major works, to show how
and why he continues to be so influential and important to
society today.

"this is an excellent place to start exploring the life and work of
probably the most celebrated dramatist not only in Britain but
also throughout the world." - Shiny New Books

www.oup.com/vsi